STOP SUPPORTING CAPITALISM!

START BUILDING SOCIALISM!

Stan Parker

First published in Great Britain in 2002
by
BRIDGE BOOKS
on behalf of
SPP

ISBN 0-9508010-8-9

A CIP catalogue entry for this book
is available for the British Library

Typeset, printed and bound by
Bridge Books
61 Park Avenue
Wrexham
LL12 7AW

Contents

Acknowledgements *v*
Introduction *vii*

Part I — CAPITALISM
1 From Primitive Communism to Class Society 13
2 Marx on Capitalism 21
3 Capitalism, by Its Advocates 30
4 Capitalism, by Its Reformist Supporters 36
5 Capitalism, by Its Mostly Critical Observers 44
6 Capitalism, by Its Revolutionary Opponents 52
7 Free Market or State Control? 59
8 Globalisation, Nation States and the New Technology 65
9 The Information Society: Selling the System 72
10 Environmental Degradation 83

Part II — SOCIALISM
11 A Brief History of Socialist Ideas 89
12 Marx on Socialism 99
13 Morris on Socialism 106
14 Revolution, Not Reformism 113
15 Common Ownership 121
16 Production for Use 128
17 Democratic Control 135
18 Free Access 142
19 A Future for Socialism 149
Bibliography 160
Index 172

ACKNOWLEDGEMENTS

I have been inspired to write this book by many socialists, past and present. My debt to Marx, Engels and Morris is apparent in the chapters I have devoted to their thoughts and hopes (though not without disagreement with some of their writings).

I first met the Socialist Party at its outdoor platform in Hyde Park in 1945. There were several excellent public speakers, but Tony Turner was outstanding. What a pity such orators are now, in Steve Coleman's phrase, stilled tongues. Some socialist writing is anonymous or under a pseudonym. So I have taken advantage of this by indulging in a little thinly-disguised plagiarism. Thanks, comrades!

Adam Buick read the whole text and offered mostly sensible suggestions which I adopted and a few not-so-sensible suggestions which I ignored. Bill Martin and Simon Wigley in Britain and Steve Kuhr in Australia helped me struggle with the complexities and frustrations of the computer. I much appreciate the assistance and advice given by Alister Williams in producing the book.

> Anyone who tries to draw the future in hard lines and vivid hues is a fool. The future will never sit for a portrait. It will come around a corner we never noticed, take us by surprise. And yet, foolishly, I cannot deny a vision born of indignation and hope.
>
> G. B. Leonard (1970)

Introduction

The dawn of the twenty-first century may not seem to be the most auspicious time to write a book advocating the replacement of world capitalism with world socialism. Scarcely a decade ago so-called communist regimes were overthrown by some form of market-based social democracy in several countries of Eastern Europe. Today capitalism-supporting parties (sometimes carrying the label socialist or Labour) hold sway in Western Europe, Australasia and elsewhere. In the USA there is a roughly 50:50 split between capitalism run by the Republicans and the same thing formerly (and probably again in the future) run by the Democrats. The rest of the world has regimes varying from outright dictatorships to full-fledged social democracies. With the exception of vestiges of feudalism and even slavery, capitalism rules everywhere, its hold getting stronger rather than weaker on the minds and in the actions of both leaders and led.

At the outset I must discuss two definitions. Socialism is the more complex and controversial of the two. A good dictionary will give several meanings of socialism —a bad dictionary will give only one (probably the one held by most anti-socialists, making it sound undesirable and impossible). My conception of socialism, derived from its nineteenth-century pioneers, is that it means a revolutionary change from any form of capitalism. The socialist movement is the set of ideas and institutions that make the new society possible and help to bring it nearer.

The essential features of socialism are production of goods and services solely and directly for use and not for profit; common ownership of the means of production and distribution (no exchange); democratic control of decision-making by those affected by the decisions; and free access to goods, services and experiences on the basis of reasonable and self-determined need.

Capitalism is the social, economic and political system that is presently dominant in most of the world. It grew out of feudalism about five or six centuries ago. During the twentieth century capitalism became stronger and, at least in the early part of this century, it is likely to increase in strength and pervasiveness. Its essential features are production for some form of market (with or without a degree of state control); private, state or other minority ownership of the means of wealth production and distribution and exchange; control of decision-making by elected or unelected representatives or leaders of the population; and access to most goods, services and experiences on the basis of ability to pay (some things may be free at the point of consumption).

*

The book is divided into two parts. In the first I concentrate on the past and present of capitalism, a historical and actually existing system. In the second part the emphasis moves to the future possibility of replacing capitalism with socialism at the level of world society. The socialist movement straddles past, present and future. It has a past and a present in the minds of an imaginative minority of people and in their actions and products (such as literature). I don't accept that we have had in the past, or have today, actually existing socialism anywhere. But the socialist movement has the potential to grow, and at some point to transmute into a world social system. Capitalism, and indeed private property systems generally, will not necessarily disappear, but at least they will be seriously challenged as prevailing modes of thought and ways of conducting human affairs.

I start with the evolution of society from classless primitive communism to various forms of class society: the restriction of free access in settled agricultural communities, slavery and feudalism. In all these class societies there was a ruling elite with power and a ruled mass with little or no power. Thanks to technological and organisational developments, labour became ever more productive, though its suppliers were always exploited by a privileged elite. Although capitalism — the employment of wage or salary labour — did not become widespread until the fifteenth century in certain parts of Europe, its origins are to be found in the employment of Flemish weavers as early as the tenth century.

In chapter 2 we turn to what is widely accepted as the most thorough and critical analysis of nineteenth century capitalism, that of Marx and Engels. We look at their theory of philosophy or world views, their theory of capitalism as an economic system, and we seek to evaluate the whole Marxist conspectus as far as property society is concerned. How far can we usefully draw on their work today? In what ways should we frankly admit that their ideas are either outdated or were misguided in the first place?

The next four chapters deal with how capitalism is understood and evaluated from several different perspectives. The first is that of its advocates, its enthusiastic and fairly uncritical supporters. They believe there are benefits to be derived from markets, other material benefits and psychological benefits. The market for labour benefits the capitalist class: workers will be employed only if a profit can be anticipated in doing so. Material benefits are fine for affluent workers in the First World but are denied to over 90 percent of the global population. Other, less tangible benefits are touted for capitalism (such as giving us the chance to express ourselves) but they are opportunities closed to all but a privileged minority.

Chapter 4 deals with the views of those who accept the basics of the system but think it can be improved. Some want to extend the scope of markets, others want to curb their excesses. Some don't like the extremes of poverty and riches they see increasing, others would like there to be more democracy. There is a constant tension between economic efficiency and welfare: getting as much out of workers as possible, but sacrificing some profit to keep them fit and happy (an uphill battle). The populist third way, or communitarianism, boils down to keeping the system intact by rejecting its extremes of cut-throat and state-controlled capitalism.

In chapter 5 we move to what I am tempted to call a growing industry: that of researching the injustices of the present system without holding out any real hope that it can or should be replaced. Perhaps I do some of these critics an injustice: deep down they may be revolutionaries without telling anyone. They critically examine commercialisation and consumerism, inequalities, change within the system, the fact that it is now ubiquitous and virtually unchallenged, the persistence of the class struggle and the destructive nature of competition.

The fourth group who have a distinctive approach to capitalism are its revolutionary opponents. At present small in number and consequently weak in influence, they argue that capitalism should not be supported in any of its forms and that its replacement by a fundamentally different form of society (socialism) should be an immediate and not just a long-term aim. These critics fall into two main groups: the avowed revolutionaries who identify with the socialist movement (primarily political, but not in the sense of wanting power to impose socialism on people who do not understand or want it) and the academic revolutionaries who seek to discuss and disseminate relevant ideas. The boundary between the two groups is flexible.

Chapter 7 looks in more detail at a question already touched on in previous chapters, that of whether capitalism should be run primarily as a free-market or a state-controlled economy. First we deal with what has often been called actually existing socialism but which is better understood as actually existing state capitalism. Then, on looking more closely at the practice of free markets, we see that markets are subject to some degree of control, whether by the state or other means. Rather than infringing the freedom of the market, the state (public sector) in many ways smoothes the path and helps to solve the problems of the private sector.

Another much-touted opposition is between the process of globalisation and the alleged decline of the nation state. Again, it is more a matter of co-operation than conflict. Certainly multinational corporations have grown in number and size, but the idea that capitalism is essentially a world system is nothing new. Nation states, rather than having become the victims of economic globalisation, are more likely to be its willing and needed partners. We also consider the extent to which the new technology (particularly information and communication technology) has contributed to a make-believe world in which experiences are increasingly sold as commodities.

In chapter 9 we continue the theme of information society, noting the various interlocking ways in which the prevailing system is sold to the general population. It starts with education, in which we are taught a set of behaviours and an ideology of compliance. The mass media play their indispensable part: owned and controlled by a tiny minority, they tell us what to think and what to buy. Hegemony is the process by which the ideas of the dominant class are disseminated to, and accepted by, the subject class: capitalism is no longer *their* system but *our* system. A culture of consumption is offered as a context in which we can achieve happiness and a sense of self.

The last chapter in Part I is concerned with the extent of damage to the environment for which capitalism is largely responsible. Problems such as global warming, greenhouse gas emissions and pollution are made worse by the favouring of short-term profit above long-term sustainability. There is, of course, a strong and growing green movement seeking to educate people about the environment and to take remedial action, but much of it is within the present system - green but not red. The general worsening of the situation strongly suggests that measures to tackle the various problems need to be taken in the context of comprehensive, revolutionary change — green *and* red.

In Part II we turn from the present to the possible future, and we start by tracing the history of socialist ideas. The word socialism dates only from the 1830s but the idea goes back much further than that. Socialism is rooted in the age-old struggle for freedom and equality. John Ball advocated common ownership during the Peasants Revolt of 1381. There followed among others the Levellers and the Diggers, the early utopians and the Paris Commune. We look at some of the literary contributions: Oscar Wilde and Jack London on capitalism, the socialist future imagined by LeGuin. The final section deals with the enemies of socialism who pretend to be its friends.

Separate chapters are devoted to the socialist ideas of Karl Marx and William Morris. Marx refused to write recipes for future cookshops but in fact his predictions about socialist society are highly significant if disappointingly few. Morris based much of his future socialist world (*News from Nowhere*) on Marx's ideas, although it also had a somewhat anarchist flavour. His prediction of how the change came — a campaign of violence by the working class against the violent state — reflected recent events when he wrote in 1890, but is today surely unacceptable. However, his depiction of life in a future stable socialist world is unrivalled in its humanity, in what it means to be a good and fulfilled citizen instead of an exploited producer and a manipulated consumer.

Chapter 14 assembles the arguments for revolution and against reformism. It is easier to get support for small changes today than for fundamental changes in the future. The possibilists have traditionally outnumbered the impossibilists, but at some point history moves on and the system does change. Often the reformists appeal to the revolutionaries to join them in left unity. But for the revolutionary it is always a poisoned chalice. Join us today, say the reformists, in our campaign for immediate improvement, and tomorrow we'll join the revolution. But tomorrow never comes. Worse still, the revolutionary movement is excluded from the agenda. The choice is now said to be not between capitalism and socialism but of what kind of capitalism we can accept.

The next four chapters attempt to summarise the basics of a future socialist world. First, common ownership of the means of wealth production and distribution, which is contrasted with the private or state ownership featured in capitalism. With socialism all people will stand equally in relation to ownership of the means of production. There will be no classes, but some goods and services will effectively be 'owned' by individuals, while larger items will be held in common. There will be no nation states, wars, armed and police forces, but any residual crime will be dealt with humanely.

In chapter 16 we outline what is implied by production solely for use, not in pursuit of profit. Needs will be met in different ways according to climate, location, availability of natural resources, individual or group preferences. Employment only to serve capitalism — useless and destructive activities of many kinds — won't be needed. This will free people for work that is not only useful but pleasurable — more like leisure. Organisation and communication will be more horizontal than vertical, people working together rather than giving or taking orders. The short-term perspective prevalent in capitalism will give way to planning and decision-making according to different time perspectives as appropriate.

Chapter 17 deals with various issues connected with democratic control of social processes. The introduction of socialism will be the work of a democratic majority. Its 'establishment' will take much longer than a day. Whereas capitalism emphasises competition, socialism will emphasise co-operation, although some benign forms of competition are likely to continue. Capitalism's professional politicians will disappear, replaced by socialist citizen delegates and representatives at various levels of decision-making. The power of leaders to control the thinking and behaviour of their followers will give way in socialism to encouragement for everyone to participate. Instead of being at the mercy of the capitalist media, socialism will have its own media.

The fourth theme of socialism is free access, each determining their own needs in the context of the society in which they will be living. There should be no problem about meeting basic needs, but 'luxuries' may require volunteers or self-production. Giving and taking will replace buying, selling and exchange. In the absence of money, calculation in kind will be used to decide the most efficient use of resources. A stock control system (already developed in capitalism) will ensure free access to goods, but other methods may be needed for services. A broad-based education for all will replace capitalist job training for the masses and elite education for the privileged.

Finally, chapter 19 is by way of summary and drawing overall conclusions. The socialist revolution will be comprehensive, affecting every part of the social fabric. Capitalism is immensely strong and its overthrow is a long-term project. Socialism is not only about what kind of social system we should have - it is also about what kind of people will develop and inhabit it. Some outline vision of the future is needed to inspire and to energise. Three controversial questions may be posed. Can we reasonably claim that socialism is a practical alternative? Who or what is our enemy? Does capitalism have a future? Though its perspective is long-term, revolution is also a sensible short-term policy. Once seriously challenged, capitalism can only respond by offering concessions in the direction of socialism.

Part I — CAPITALISM

Chapter 1

FROM PRIMITIVE COMMUNISM TO CLASS SOCIETY

Compared with a lion, a gorilla, or even a horse, the human animal is weak, slow and defenceless. And yet homo sapiens has become the dominant species of the planet. Our species developed none of the specialised attributes that have fitted other creatures so well for their environments. Physiologically, we have hardly evolved at all since we became a distinct species. Whereas other species have evolved to fit their environments and the available food supplies, human beings have remained unspecialised, but very adaptable. Instead of their bodies altering to suit their environments, they have altered their environments to suit themselves.

Human beings spread across the surface of the planet, occupying tropical rain forests, deserts, temperate regions, and even polar ice. They lived on virtually every type of food possible, from seal fat to tropical fruits and desert insects. And from this variety of life-patterns there arose wide differences in knowledge, beliefs, attitudes, feelings and behaviour. Almost every conceivable kind of belief has been adopted by some humans at some time somewhere. Although we are one species, from the jungle of New Guinea to the streets of New York, the inhabitants of different places may think and act in quite dissimilar ways.

And yet a baby, carried across the world from New Guinea to New York and brought up there, could become a complete New Yorker, with the accent, the food preferences, the personal habits, the love of baseball, and the average tendency towards obesity, heart disease, divorce and crime. The basic animal is the same, but all behaviour patterns and ideas are shaped by the society in which the child is brought up.

But if societies mould individuals, different types of society are themselves shaped by a number of external factors, as well as by the activities of individuals and classes within them. The basic needs of the human animal are, like those of any other mammal, food, drink, warmth and sex. But these needs have not always been easily met. For most of human existence, the lives of the great majority have been dominated by scarcity. The methods of making a living from the land and sea have therefore been the major influences on the sorts of lives people have led, the types of society that have been formed, and the attitudes and behaviour of those societies.

We do not know exactly how long ago human beings evolved from other species. Modern man, according to many anthropologists, emerged in Africa about 100,000 years ago, and gradually spread out from there to replace all earlier species in the rest of the world (Snooks, 1996:50). For most of that time people lived communally, through hunting and gathering. For many thousands of years there was no private property, no money, no working for wages, no stock exchange and no class divisions. People lived with and for one another. It was a system of primitive communism.

The comic cartoon idea of the cave man with his club displaying aggression towards everyone is a fiction. Such an individual would not have lasted a week in the world of prehistory. Human beings have survived and prospered because they are adaptable and they have co-operated with one another. Long before there were private property societies with their class divisions and exploitation, small hunter-gatherer communities relied for their existence on all members playing their part. This co-operation lasted for many tens of thousands of years. The remnants of it can still be seen in surviving primitive communities such as of the Bushmen of the Kalahari Desert, the pygmies of the Congo rain forests, Australian aborigines and South American Indians.

The earliest human societies — as self-sufficient producer groups — would have been composed of relatively small numbers whose members survived in nature as nomadic bands capturing and killing wild animals and gathering wild plants, fruits and insects. The particular character of these material conditions of production demanded a certain division of labour between hunters, gatherers and those engaged in making the tools used in these activities. They also demanded free access to nature, the main means of production.

Thus, in accordance with the material conditions of production in which hunter-gatherer societies operated, they were societies which did not know private ownership of the means of production. There was no private ownership of what was produced. What was produced — whether by hunting or gathering — was not the private property of the hunter or the hunting party or of the gatherer(s) but was to be shared out among all the members of the group on an equitable basis. Hunting, gathering and tool-making were all regarded as essential activities entitling those who performed them to be maintained by the whole group.

It used to be thought that living by hunting and gathering was a bad way to live. But recent evidence suggests that they lived in surprisingly abundant environments that provided all of the basic calories, nutrients and proteins they needed, and they worked relatively few hours to enjoy those things. This left them plenty of free time for visiting relatives, playing games, or just relaxing (Sanderson, 1995:21).

Anthropologists who live among the hunter-gatherers who survive today describe the ways in which they are generally free from material pressures. According to Sahlins:

> It is not that hunters and gatherers have curbed their materialistic impulses; they simply never made an institution of them... We are inclined to think of hunters and gatherers as poor because they don't have anything; perhaps better to think of them as free. A good case can be made that hunters and gatherers work less than we do; and, rather than a continuous travail, the food quest is intermittent, leisure abundant, and there is a greater amount of sleep in the daytime per capita per year than in any other condition of society (1972:14)

Settled agriculture

The practice of settled agriculture represented a major change in the material conditions of production. It meant an end to nomadism and the establishment of settled communities. It also meant an increase in the amount of food available, so permitting an increase in the size of human communities. But it also involved a different division of labour which paved the way, as it developed, for the emergence of minority control over access to the means of production.

The first settled agricultural communities would have been established by societies which had previously practised hunting and gathering and so had a communistic economic structure. This was characterised by the absence of private ownership of the means of production and by the sharing of products according to need. After the adoption of agriculture, these communistic economic arrangements survived for a while, but tended to break down in the long run as they no longer corresponded to the material conditions of production.

The social arrangement for meeting the material requirements of early agriculture is most likely to have been the allocation to family units of plots of land to cultivate. This was not yet the establishment of private ownership, but it meant the end of free access to the means of production that had obtained in hunter-gatherer societies. It ruled out any member of society simply helping themselves to the products of any plot of land. Normally they would only have free access to the products of the plot cultivated by the family unit to which they belonged.

Nevertheless, such a limitation is not incompatible with the continuation of some communistic practices. The actual cultivators could still be regarded by the community as performing a function on its behalf and be required by social custom to contribute any surplus product to a common store on which any member in need could draw. This could happen, for instance, as a result of their crops having failed or been destroyed by a storm. Such social arrangements have been discovered in societies at this stage of development which have survived into modern times.

The existence of a common store becomes another aspect of the society's material conditions of production and requires a social arrangement for managing this store, collecting and distributing the surpluses. The usual arrangement seems to have been to confer this responsibility on a particular family. Arguments can go on as to whether being given this responsibility was conferred on a family whose head had already acquired this status for other reasons, perhaps military or religious. But the fact remains that this role of collecting and redistributing surpluses had to be filled if all the members of the community were able to meet their basic needs as of right.

The emergence of class society

It is easy to imagine how over time the co-ordinating role in distribution could become a source of privileged consumption for the chief and his family. The duty to contribute any surplus products to the common storehouse could become a duty to contribute this to the chief, and the chief and his family could come to consume an excessive amount of the stores at the expense of distributing them to those in need.

The tendency for what was originally a necessary technical function to evolve into a social privilege would have been even more pronounced when the co-ordinating role concerned production rather than simply distribution. It was the case when large-scale irrigation works had to be managed so that agriculture could be practised. For instance, this happened with agriculture in the Nile, Euphrates and other river valleys. It was the main material condition of production which gave rise to an economic structure in which the cultivators were exploited by a class of priests who collectively controlled the key means of production which the irrigation works represented.

The emergence of control over means of production by a section of society, or social class, was a radical departure in human social arrangements. Production was no longer controlled by society as a whole. Such societies ceased to be communities with a common interest and became divided, with one class, on the basis of its control over access to and use of the material forces of production, exploiting the productive work of the other class and allocating itself a privileged consumption.

The emergence of class and property meant that some humans acquired the power to exclude others from access to the material forces of production, including nature, except on their terms. In these circumstances, humans ceased to be a united community seeking to satisfy the needs of all its members. Instead they became members of a class-divided society in which there is internal conflict over how the material forces of production and distribution should be used: to satisfy the needs of all or to accumulate wealth for the few.

Throughout history this conflict has nearly always been settled in favour of the class that has controlled the means of production. There are two main reasons for this. First, the power of this class was based on a real functional role within the division of labour, at least originally. Secondly, this class controlled armed bodies to enforce its will, thus enabling it to hold on to power, at least for a while, even after its original function in organising production had disappeared and been taken over by some other group as a result of technological change.

The discovery and utilisation of metals, and the development of more and more complex tools and machines have usually gone hand in hand with progress in methods of making a living, increasing the amount of wealth produced per capita many times over. But the benefits of these improvements have not been shared by all members of society. After the rise of settled townships on an agricultural base in Mesopotamia, trade between localities developed. For the first time the products of hands and brains took on an alien life as commodities to be bartered, and then bought and sold with the abstract commodity of money. Property, realised at the boundary between tribes, began to impinge within them. The first property society came to be developed when people were bought and sold as slaves.

Slavery

Slavery differs fundamentally from wage labour. With the wage system the labour power of the worker becomes one of the main commodities in the marketplace. With slavery the workers themselves become commodities, they have no rights and are legally the property of the person who controls them. Slaves were fundamental to the economy of ancient Greece and Rome during their classical periods — the fifth to third centuries BC for Greece and the first century BC to the second century AD for Rome (Applebaum, 1992:170).

Anyone might have become a slave through capture in war, piracy, or breaking the law. They could be bought or sold through the slave trade on the open market. Slaves in theory had no rights. They were property and might be disposed of as their masters wished. In practice, slaves did have some protection under the law — the owner could not maltreat slaves or put them to death with impunity.

Access to political power was unthinkable for slaves. The only form of action they could take was running away when a favourable opportunity arose. However, it cannot be assumed that all slaves occupied a low status in Greek and Roman society, although undoubtedly most of them did. Slaves worked on farms, in workshops and in mines, mostly under harsh conditions. But there were slaves employed as managers and administrators, especially during the Roman Empire. Slaves were also employed as professionals, teachers, doctors, and household servants. Some slaves who were engaged in commerce even engaged their own slaves.

Between 1500 and 1870 plantations in the southern USA, the Caribbean and Brazil contained 10 million slaves (Wallace, 1990:71). Although it is mainly an institution of the past, slavery or slave-like practices are still common around the world (Levinson and Christensen, 1996:291). The three main forms are child labour, debt bondage and forced labour. Around 100 million children world-wide are forced to work long hours in unhealthy conditions and are paid little or nothing for their labour. In India alone an estimated 6.5 million people have pledged their labour against debts. Often the debt bondage (illegal since 1976) remains so for life.

Feudalism

In the feudal system absolute ownership of the land is vested in the feudal lord but, unlike the slave owner, his title to the worker (serf) is not absolute. The lord owns him merely by title to a share of his labour. In return he is obligated to grant the worker use of some land, some ownership of tools and some of the products of his own labour. Slavery thus gave way to serfdom. In both cases the majority was exploited by the minority. The slave owned none of the products of his labour but was fed and clothed by his owner. The serf had enough to keep himself and his family alive, but the rest was appropriated by the lord, a non-producer (Venable, 1945:100).

Feudalism evolved as a hierarchical system of personal relationships in which land and military power — and of course the labour of the serfs — were the principal commodities exchanged. (Singman 1999:4). The system was strengthened and expanded in Britain with the eleventh-century Norman Conquest. In feudal times the king nominally owned all the land. He granted lands to his tenants-in-chief, the aristocracy, and they in return had to give military service to him and pay customary dues which comprised a percentage of their wealth. Not only did the feudal aristocracy and the church own most of the land, but they controlled the men and women who lived and worked on it. The landlords had their own courts, they levied taxes and exacted services from their serfs and, in times of war, they ordered their subjects to fight their battles.

The power of the feudal lord depended on the amount of land he owned and the number of peasants he could control. Peasants had feudal obligations to their landlord. They either had to work on his land for a certain length of time each week or else they had to give him a portion of their produce in return for living on his land. Either way, the landlord received his wealth without having to work.

Every family had access to a piece of land for cultivation and to the commons for pasturing their animals. Their rights were recognised by all. The behaviour which regulated society was not backed by sanctions — law, police or army — but by custom which was a condition of existence: expulsion from the community could mean death from hunger or exposure (Smith, 1994:58).

Capitalist social relations emerged with the expropriation of common land by the aristocracy in the fifteenth and sixteenth centuries. The lands were enclosed to be used for sheep farming rather than arable cultivation. One reason for this was that the new Flemish woollen industry made sheep more profitable tenants than peasants. Enclosure destroyed the lives of thousands of peasant families, turning them into propertyless vagabonds. In dealing with the primitive accumulation of capital, Marx wrote:

> The fathers of the present working class were chastised for their enforced transformation into vagabonds and paupers. Legislation treated them as voluntary criminals and assumed that it depended on their own good will to go on working under the old conditions that no longer existed (1954, vol. 1 :686).

Deprived of their land, their homes, their traditional surroundings and the protection of the law, the expropriated peasantry were left to sell the one thing they possessed — their ability to work. The introduction of wage labour was the starting point of capitalism.

Chapter 2

MARX ON CAPITALISM

The main aim of this chapter is to present an appreciative and critical account of the contribution of Marx and Engels to the critique of capitalism. What they had to say about socialism — how to achieve it and what it will be like — I shall defer to chapter 12. Neither chapter will deal with the Marxism that has been developed by various writers, leaders, parties and movements that have interpreted, extended, and in some cases distorted the writings of Marx and Engels for their own purposes.

The chapter is divided into three parts: (1) the Marxian theory of philosophy (the general or world views of Marx and Engels), (2) their theory of capitalism, a critical analysis of the profit system, mainly from an economic standpoint, and (3) an examination of the Marxian conspectus, paying particular attention to points of similarity and difference between the views of Marx/Engels and those of socialists today.

Theory

I shall use the term theory here broadly to include ideas, thoughts, values, hypotheses, propositions — even predictions if they are part of a system of thought. It will be convenient to divide the discussion into two separate but related parts: philosophy (the general or world views of Marx and Engels) and capitalism (their critical analysis of the profit system, mainly from an economic standpoint). Two further parts of Marxist theory — politics (how they see the revolutionary change from capitalism to socialism/communism taking place) and socialism (their conception of the major features of the new society) — will be deferred to chapter 12.

To seek an understanding of Marxist theory is at first sight a formidable task. The sheer size of the project — the total writings of Marx and Engels have been estimated at between 6 and 7 million words — is daunting. When compounded by the fact that much of their expression is far from simple, the project is not an easy one. Yet it may reasonably be claimed that Marxism is not inherently difficult to understand, in either its philosophic or economic aspects (Sowell, 1985: 13). We need to sort out the wood from the trees, and to recognise that some of the trees are dead stumps left over from past polemics whose relevance to the world today has long gone.

The central concepts of Marxist philosophy are scientific socialism, dialectics, materialism (divided into dialectical and historical), and the blending of structure and action. There are other ways of analysing the components of Marxist philosophy, but that is the approach I shall take here.

Marx acknowledged the contribution to his own scientific philosophy of Hegel, the economics of Ricardo and the utopian socialism of Fourier, St Simon, Owen and others. He saw utopian socialism as idealistic, not in the popular sense of unselfish thought and action in the service of a better society, but in the sense of an ideal society projected into the future and unconnected with existing social trends.

Marx's scientific method was to proceed by simplifying concrete and complex manifestations into an abstraction, which becomes less and less complex until we get at the simplest conception. Then, by systematically adding complicating factors, we start on our return journey towards empirical reality as a rich aggregate of many conceptions and realities (Marx, 1904: 292-3). In short, Marx believed in abstraction, systematic analysis, and successive approximations to a reality too complex to grasp directly (Sowell, 1985: 18).

Concerning dialectical materialism, Venable (1945) has a useful summary of Marx and Engels on the question of relating it to other forms of materialism:

> ...dialectical materialism, their naturalistic philosophy of change and interaction; historical materialism, their theory of social and cultural transformation and of the interactive, emergent, and progressive character of history's movement; economic materialism, an elaborate subdivision of, or rather basis for, their social theory.

The dialectical component of dialectical materialism concerns the inadequacy of all polar opposites and using the dialectical method to overcome that inadequacy. A well-known formulation is the confrontation of an initial thesis by an antithesis, resulting in a new thesis which preserves what is of value in both. Thus capitalism consists of the thesis of social production confronted by the antithesis of individual appropriation and private property, to be overcome by the socialist synthesis of wealth produced socially, distributed according to need not profit, and held in common. For Marx the material interchange between man and nature is the basic form of dialectic (McLellan, 1971:154).

Marx's theory of historical materialism is based on the simple proposition that production is the first premise of all human existence: people must first be in a position to live in order to be able to make history (quoted in Thomas, 1998:6). The theory attempts to explain the transformation of whole societies from one era to another. It sees the source of these changes in changing technologies (productive relations) which bring changes in the way people are organised (social relations) (Sowell, 1985:70). Engels expands on this:

> The materialist conception of history starts from the principle that production, and with production the exchange of its products, is the basis of every social order; that in every society which has appeared in history the distribution of the products, and with it the division of society into classes or estates, is determined by what is produced, and how the product is exchanged (1936:300).

For Marx, humans are neither the passive products of their circumstances nor at liberty to fashion their circumstances at will: 'Men make their own history, but they do not make it just as they please; they do not make it under circumstances chosen by themselves, but under circumstances directly encountered, given and transmitted from the past' (Marx, 1935:300).

Marxian theory implies a blending of structure and action. We need to understand how Marx sought to bridge the concerns of both philosophy and science in developing a theory that operates simultaneously at the levels of structure and action. We need to take into account the philosophic critique of consciousness, the scientific analysis of capitalist economic institutions, and the historical study of politics and society. Furthermore, the Marxian priority is with action rather than philosophy or the study of structures. One of their most famous aphorisms is that the point is not to study society but to change it.

Capitalism

The second area of Marxist theory is their analysis of capitalism. To do thoroughly this would be a very complex undertaking indeed. So I shall start with a relatively short statement of Marx's general theory of capitalism:

> The core of the capitalist system, according to Marx, is found in how the propertyless proletariat must sell its labour power to those who have

> accumulated capital... Exploitation of the worker occurred because the capitalists derived a surplus through the workers' creation of commodities whose value was greater than the value the workers received for their labour services (under normal conditions and in the long run). Whenever it was profitable to do so, the capitalist introduced technological improvements into the production process, which took the form of labour-saving devices.
>
> Technologically-displaced labour became, according to Marx, part of the reserve army of unemployed. The existence of this surplus pool of labour, competing for available jobs, kept wages close to a social subsistence level... the consuming power of the working class was held down. At the same time, the capitalists restricted their own present consumption so as to accumulate more capital... adding to society's productive capacity and subsequently to its reserve army of unemployed... In addition the intimate relation between the capital goods sector and the consumer goods sector gets disrupted. These are the basic internal economic contradictions in the capitalist system. Marx said that this leads to depressions, imperialism, wars, and a class struggle of ever-increasing severity (Leiman, 1970:321).

That statement links together several of Marx's concepts in compiling a critical account of capitalism: labour power, exploitation, surplus value, unemployment, consumption, capital accumulation, depressions, wars and class struggle. We may go on to look more closely at three of what are arguably the main concepts of Marxian economics: the labour theory of value, the commodity nature of production, and classes and class struggle.

Marx's labour theory of value, together with his ideas about the commodity nature of capitalist production, seek to explain how the profit system works and how the working class is exploited under that system. First some (simplified) definitions. Wealth is anything useful produced by human labour from materials found in nature. In capitalism wealth takes the form of an immense accumulation of commodities. A commodity is an article of wealth produced for the purpose of being exchanged for other articles of wealth. The means of production (land, factories, railways, *etc.*) become capital when used to exploit labour (human energy) to produce surplus value (profit). Money is capital in its pure form. The capitalist invests capital and buys labour power to produce commodities to be sold at a profit. Finally, price is the monetary expression of value. Some things that are bought and sold are either not products of labour or sell at prices disproportionate to the amount of labour embodied in them, for example land and objects of art. But these exceptions do not invalidate the labour theory of value as of general applicability.

Gibson-Graham (1996:3) describes what he calls the Marxist vision of capitalism:

> ... a system of generalised commodity production structured by (industrial) forces of production and exploitative production relations between capital and labour. Workers, bereft of means of production, sell their labour power for wages and participate in the labour process under capitalist control. Their surplus labour is appropriated by capitalists as surplus value. The capitalist mode of production is animated by the twin imperatives of enterprise competition and capital accumulation, which together account for the dynamic tendencies of capitalism to expand and to undergo recurring episodes of crisis.

The Marxian theory of class and class struggle offers an explanation of capitalist production. A class is made up of people who are in the same position in relation to the ownership and control of the means of wealth production. For Marx and Engels the class struggle between the bourgeoisie (capitalist class) and the proletariat (working class) is the great lever of modem social change. Originally Marx identified three classes on the basis of source of income: wage for labour, profit for the capitalist and rent for the landowner. But capitalism has now succeeded in absorbing the major landlords into the elite, leaving society polarised between two classes, capitalists and workers.

The Marxian theory of class is opposed by those academics and others who explain class not in terms of ownership or non-ownership of the means of production, but in terms such as those of prestige and style of life. Society is said to consist of a hierarchy of non-conflicting classes, with names such as upper, middle, working and under. Such an approach tends to gloss over the fact that only about two percent of the population own enough capital to live comfortably on the income it provides. The other 98 percent have to find an employer, be dependent on someone else or live off state benefit. In some countries even the latter is not available.

Brief mention should be made of a few other Marxian ideas relating to the analysis of capitalism. Marx is sometimes associated with the belief that as capitalism continues it will lead to the increasing misery of the working class. His use of the term misery should be taken as relative to the condition of the capitalist class, not absolute:

> ...although the enjoyments of the worker have risen, the social satisfaction that they give has fallen in comparison with the increased enjoyments of the

> capitalist. Our desires and pleasures spring from society, we measure them, therefore, by society and not by the objects which serve for their satisfaction. Because they are of a social nature, they are of a relative nature (Marx and Engels, 1868:94).

Alienation is a concept much discussed by Marx but relatively neglected in commentaries on Marxism. The alienation of the worker under capitalism is divided by Marx into four aspects:

> The worker is related to the product of his labour as to an alien object. The object he produces does not belong to him, dominates him, and only serves in the long run to increase his poverty. Alienation appears not only in the result, but also in the process of production and productive activity itself. The worker is not at home in his work which he views only as a means of satisfying other needs. It is an activity directed against himself, that is independent of him and does not belong to him. Thirdly, alienated labour succeeds in alienating man from his species. Species life, productive life, life creating life, turns into a mere means of sustaining the worker's individual existence, and man is alienated from his fellow men. Finally, nature itself is alienated from man, who thus loses his own inorganic body (Marx, quoted in McLellan, 1971:119).

McLellan makes it clear that Marx conceived the state of alienation to be common to all members of capitalist society, not just the workers. The propertied class may feel comfortable in their ability to exercise power over the workers, but they are no more free from the inhumanity of the capitalist system than the jailer is free from the restrictions of the prison regime.

A concept allied to alienation is what Marx called the fetishism of commodities. Workers are dominated by the products of their own activities but do not realise this and attribute an independent existence and power to those products:

> ... the existence of things as commodities, and the value-relation between the products of labour which stamps them as commodities, have absolutely no connection with their physical properties and with the material relations arising therefrom. There is a definite social relation between men that assumes in their eyes the fantastic form of a relation between things. This I call the Fetishism which attaches itself to the products of labour as soon as they are produced as commodities, and which is therefore inseparable from the production of commodities (Marx, 1954:77).

Evaluation

Well over a century after they were writing, how should we evaluate the contribution of Marx and Engels to our understanding of a system that, during the intervening period, has seen many changes, though arguably not fundamental changes? How far can socialists today usefully draw on their work? In what ways should be frankly admit that their ideas are either outdated or were misguided in the first place?

First their philosophical view. I have no doubt that socialists should continue today, as they have done in the past, to regard the immense sweep and authority of Marxist thought as extremely valuable in the task of replacing capitalism with socialism. Neither Marx nor Engels were specialists in the sense of concentrating on any one aspect of society or the movement towards socialism. They wrote, sometimes in a very detailed way, on economics but they were not primarily economists. They were interested in the history of humankind through all its stages of development from primitive communism to capitalism, but their history was not merely academic — it was for a revolutionary purpose.

Because science, meaning accumulated systematic knowledge, has expanded in all fields so greatly since Marx's time, the claim that his greatest contribution was as a scientist needs to be treated with caution. Singer's assessment seems more valid: 'It is better to think of Marx as a philosopher — in the broadest sense — rather than as a scientist... As a philosopher, Marx's work endures. It has altered our understanding of our own nature, and deepened our grasp of what it is to be free.' (1980:68).

A second Marxist concern was with the analysis of capitalism. In the time since Marx and Engels were writing, capitalism has changed drastically, though not fundamentally. It is sometimes claimed that Marx's analysis of capitalism dealt — and in fact could only have dealt — with the capitalism of his time. We may acknowledge that limitation, while recognising the tremendous contribution that Marx did make to understanding the nature of capitalism as a system, with essential features that are as evident today as when he was writing. Wood makes such a balanced judgement:

> It is fair enough to say that a body of work produced to deal with capitalism in the nineteenth century cannot be adequate to the conditions of the twentieth. But it is a great deal less self-evident that anything else has emerged in the interim which provides a better foundation — or even one remotely as good — for a critical analysis of capitalism (1995:3).

A good example of Marx's remarkable anticipation of the direction of capitalist development is the following passage on what is usually referred to as globalisation:

> The need of a constantly expanding market for its profits chases the bourgeoisie over the whole surface of the globe. The bourgeoisie has through its exploitation of the world market given a cosmopolitan character to production and consumption... In place of the old wants, satisfied by the production of the country, we now find new wants, requiring for their satisfaction the products of distant lands and climes. In place of the old local and national seclusion and self-sufficiency, we have intercourse in every direction, universal inter-dependence of nations (1848:5).

Capitalism is still a system of human exploitation, still one in which commodity production alienates us from what we produce — and even from ourselves. With some justification it may be argued that Marx was less concerned about poverty than about alienation. Without downplaying the suffering and deprivation caused by material poverty, we should also recognise the abjectly poor quality of life that capitalism offers most of its supporters. Think of rush-hour sardine-tin-like mass public transport, the eminently throw-away tabloid newspapers, the excruciatingly dumbed-down TV shows — and much more.

Most critics of Marxist economics believe in capitalism. Some of them are happy to applaud Marx's analysis of where power lies in capitalist society but are opposed to overthrowing that society. However, it is possible to criticise some of Marx's views on capitalism while supporting his call to abolish it. Thus Stratman criticises Marx for relying on the self-interest of the working class:

> Though it is destined to act as the agent of revolution, in Marx's paradigm the working class puts an end to human exploitation not as a conscious goal on behalf of all humanity, but as the inevitable by-product of ending its own exploitation. It accomplishes the general interest of humanity by acting in its own self-interest (n.d.:166).

Working-class pursuit of its own self-interest has so far led only to trade unionism, not socialism. As we have seen, Marx and Engels did support any revolutionary movement against the existing society and political order of things. They did not qualify this support by insisting that it be based on socialist/communist understanding rather than on mere reaction against a class of exploiters. They paid the price for this in disillusion when uprisings such as the Paris Commune failed to spark the introduction of classless society.

The Marxist analysis of capitalism has been the victim of two historical forces. Bolshevism and the various expressions of Leninism and Trotskyism allowed opponents of Marxism to give life to the argument that oppression and compulsion lay at the heart of the Marxian prescription. Much more damaging for Marxism, though, was the social-democratic age. Social democracy was and is based on the simple proposition that capitalism has changed for the better, tamed by the unions but who must not be given too much power by Labour governments (Haseler, 2000).

Chapter 3

CAPITALISM, BY ITS ADVOCATES

This is the first of four chapters which consider various manifestations of contemporary capitalism from different points of view. Here we discuss how people who advocate the system see it and why they think it is better than any alternative (including not accepting that there is any alternative). Subsequent chapters deal with capitalism's reformist supporters, its mostly critical observers, and its revolutionary opponents.

Since capitalism is what most of the world has in some form at present, it possesses all the advantages of being the status quo. It is easy to accept that the arrangements, structures and ideas that prevail now are the normal and natural way of doing things — the only way if you have no sense of history and no imagination. To stay where you are is much easier than to move somewhere else, whether physically or mentally. To seek change is to take a risk that the unknown will be worse than the known — better the devil you know than the devil you don't.

In this chapter I aim to review some of the significant claims that have been made about the virtues and benefits of capitalism and about the dangers of getting rid of it. Somewhat arbitrarily, I divide the benefits that have been put forward into three groups: those of the market, those relating to other material benefits, and those of a more psychological or intangible nature. These benefits are not really separate — they are often seen to be mutually reinforcing. Writers who draw attention to one kind of benefit would probably agree that the other kinds also apply, perhaps with less emphasis.

Benefits of the market

The virtues of capitalism are often linked with the benefits that the market system — buying, selling and exchanging — has brought to the human race. The market is easily idolised, even worshipped, as a marvellous, albeit mysterious mechanism, with a life of its own that works best when tampered with least. The invisible hand of the market is said to wave genially over the fortuitous coming together of a willing buyer and a willing seller.

Seldon puts the case for capitalism in the following glowing terms:

> ...capitalism emerges in markets official and unofficial, legal or illegal, in socialist as well as capitalist economies, because it is the instrument which people in all societies and stages or economic development instinctively use to escape from want and enrich one another by exchange... And the market is a capitalist instrument that requires the responsible private opportunities and rewards, the risks and penalties of individual ownership and judgement, not a socialist instrument subject to the irresponsible mercurial collective decisions of public men or women who control other people's resources but are ultimately compelled, like the rest of fallible mankind, to put their personal interests first (1990:1).

Forget the reference to socialist economies. He is referring to places like the former Soviet Union which had a state-controlled rather than a relatively free market form of capitalism (more on this in chapter 7). Note that we are said to enrich one another by exchange. But only if we own what we exchange and deny others access to any surplus we may have. If I own capital and you own only your labour power, then clearly neither of us will get enriched if you refuse to let me exploit you by employing you to make a surplus for me. Buying and selling is not possible without exchange. But the exchange does not have to be fair to both sides. This is particularly the case with the labour market. You market your labour and if you are lucky you find a buyer for it. But the exchange won't take place if the employer can't see a profit in employing you. So much for the one-sided benefits accruing to participants in the labour market.

The capitalist market system is nothing if not sophisticated, and there is evidence that it is becoming more so. Its advocates point to this sophistication as a benefit:

> The market is no longer that cold, implacable and impersonal monster which imposes its laws and procedures while extending them even further. It is a many-sided, diversified, evolving device which the social sciences as well as the actors themselves contribute to reconfigure (Callon, 1998:51).

A not unattractive word picture, but does it correspond to contemporary reality? Using the same logic, Callon would no doubt reply to a complainant about cold weather that it was colder still in the ice age. In talking up the nice and non-monstrous things about the market today, Callon may be thinking of employees who are paid to counsel other employees who are given the sack by their common employer, and of the occasionally generous compensation awarded by courts to some employees whose health is ruined by negligent employers. As for the market being many-sided, diversified and evolving, it can certainly be all of those things, but the main beneficiaries are a privileged minority, not the vast mass of the population.

Perhaps a minor benefit of the market is to put a price on as many things as possible. No need to be squeamish about this. If you own something that is in short supply, you can put a higher price on it. Lawson, ex-Chancellor of the Exchequer, is a realist without too many moral scruples, and seems rather glad that most other supporters of capitalism think similarly: 'people well understand that any pay relates to performance, as measured in the market-place, rather than to moral worth'(1989:40).

Other material benefits

According to its more enthusiastic supporters, capitalism requires not defence but celebration: 'Its achievement in creating high and rising living standards for the masses without sacrificing personal liberties speaks for itself' (Seldon, 1990:ix). Something like 90 percent of humanity may well ask: what high and rising living standards and what liberties? In the relatively rich countries there are substantially more material benefits than in the past, but the struggle to earn the money to pay for them is as great, if not greater than, ever. In the Third World the inequalities and the absolute poverty are generally getting worse.

Seldon goes on to make a claim for capitalism that is not often made, at least not by those of its supporters who have some respect for the working class who produce the world's wealth:

> Only capitalism can make the consumer in us sovereign, and has in varying degree done so in history, because the competition of the market can prevent us from myopically asserting our interests as producers by protecting established but outdated industries, occupations and jobs (p.119).

Note the divide and rule strategy employed here. Also the double standards. Workers (95–98 percent of the population, depending on how much capital you think is needed to make a capitalist) are producers, but also consumers. The competition of the market is said to benefit consumers. No doubt it often does — statistics in economically advanced countries tend to show that many consumer items cost less in working time than in the earlier stages of capitalism. But don't forget the human costs of the outdated industries, occupations and jobs. Some capital may be lost as industries, such as coal and shipbuilding, decline, but the deprivation resulting from losses of occupations and jobs is far more tragic.

Apologists for capitalism usually invite us to measure the benefits of the system only in material terms. For Walker (1990:44) 'the strategy of inequality itself has only severely disadvantaged a substantial minority of society while ensuring rising living standards for the majority.' We are thus invited to be thankful that severe disadvantage is caused to only a substantial minority. A small price to pay, perhaps?

One of the better-known exponents of the benefits of capitalism is Margaret Thatcher. This is from one of her speeches:

> Capitalism and enterprise is a system that only works by spreading ever more widely to more and more of the population what used to be the privileges of the few. Capitalism could not exist otherwise. It gets its profits and its investment for the future by spreading to the enormous number of people the benefits, whether in terms of consumer goods or capital (Jenkins, 1988:334).

Then there is the efficiency argument. If you choose the right comparison to make, it isn't too difficult to prove that capitalism is the most efficient system known to humankind:

> ... capitalism has proven far more efficient than centrally planned economic systems in developing and utilizing technology, and in adapting to the rapidly changing conditions of a global division of labor (Fukuyama, 1992:91).

Two points here: Some forms of capitalism are more efficient in their production of goods, services and profits than others (for example, the contemporary US economy more than the former Soviet Union economy). But we must ask: efficient from whose point of view? And efficiency in production, if it is achieved at the cost of physical or mental damage to the producers, may not be a preferred option for society as a whole.

Finally, there is the material benefit that accrues to capitalists when they buy labour and use it in conjunction with capital to make a profit. This is the much vaunted partnership between capital and labour, according to which both are entitled to their reward, the one as profit, the other as wages. Sometimes there is talk of the risk and sacrifice, even the bravery, of capitalists, who take a chance that they won't make a profit — and may even make a loss. Schweikart (1993:ix) has the measure of this: 'We should admit that we cannot get beyond capitalism at this moment, not because there exists no viable, desirable beyond but because those who most profit from the present order are too powerful.'

Psychological benefits

We should not imagine that capitalism offers only material benefits to its participants. Capitalist man, keen though he may be to make a fast (or even a slow) buck, does not live by bread alone. The system is said to be good for us in less tangible ways. We may examine some variations on this theme.

Have you noticed that the market offers to each of us a way to express ourselves, because we all need our customers to reassure us that we are making a difference, are needed or wanted, appreciated or respected? You haven't noticed that? Well, Handy (1998:48) has. In fact he goes so far as to say that: 'If I could not sell my books to willing buyers, I doubt that I would want to write.' If enough of us refuse to buy books like Handy's that support capitalism, it may strike a mortal blow to the system — but don't bank on it!

A concept closely related to self-expression is creativity. Peet (1991:185) writes of capitalism's great discovery, that people freed of servile relations are creative and innovative, capable of doing almost anything. He no doubt has in mind the fortunate few who have the knack of being able to build a successful business from scratch, find a gap in the increasingly overcrowded market, or otherwise exploit the labour of others. Most of the population, however, are not free of employment, which is a form of servile relation — wage slavery. They may be potentially creative or innovative, but their need to find an employer and expend their labour, often to no useful social purpose, ensures that the only way they can feel capable of doing almost anything is by purchasing some of the mind-blowing drugs that the market pushes.

I referred earlier to the claims made in favour of contemporary capitalism by comparing it with selected other forms of society. The comparison may be with pre-capitalist societies or with one form of contemporary capitalism as allegedly superior to other forms. Novak (1982:13) makes some plausible claims for democratic capitalism:

> Of all the systems of political economy which have shaped our history, none has so revolutionized ordinary expectations of human life — lengthened the life span, made the elimination of poverty and famine thinkable, enlarged the range of human choice — as democratic capitalism.

We can agree with much of this claim, but should strongly dispute its implication that capitalism is the best of all possible systems. It *has* revolutionised ordinary expectations of human life — mostly, but far from always, for the better. People do live longer on average than they did in feudal or slave times (but the most long-lived individuals are found outside mainstream capitalist conditions, doing rural work, eating healthy foods and living in mountainous areas). It is true that inventions and improvements in productive methods have made the elimination of poverty and famine thinkable. But the challenge is to turn what is now only thinkable into reality. There is no evidence that capitalism is capable of meeting this challenge. The profit system may have enlarged the range of human choice but it hasn't enabled the numerous poor to choose escape from poverty, avoidable disease or starvation.

Chapter 4

CAPITALISM, BY ITS REFORMIST SYMPATHISERS

There are two main ways in which reforms of the capitalist system may be formulated and pursued. One is by proposing changes to the existing form of capitalism. The other concerns change from one form of capitalism to another. The latter may appear to be the more radical, but in fact both share the common feature of not standing for a fundamentally different type of society. To put this another way, both stand for a smaller or larger change to the present system. The larger changes — from state-controlled to free-market capitalism and less often the other way round — will be the subject of chapter 7. Here we shall concentrate on reforms of what are popularly known as free-market or mixed economies. If capitalism is slightly wounded in the process of being reformed, it may console itself with the thought that it is the victim only of friendly fire.

Improving or curbing the market

There is in fact no such thing as a completely free market, except in some economists' minds and textbooks. Even within largely free-market economies such as that of the contemporary United States, there is some degree of restriction of trade, some limits on what can be bought and sold, when and where, by which groups and not others, monopoly control, and so on. Much of politics consists of disputes about whether and in what ways markets should be curbed or improved. Only revolutionaries advocate the abolition of markets in all their forms and a society based on production directly to meet needs, not for profit.

We may first look at the reasoning of reformers that capitalism would work better if markets were improved by encouraging more competition. One argument is that when sellers compete, prices for buyers come down (the obverse argument, that when buyers compete, sellers get a better price, is less often used, perhaps because a prominent example of this is the buying of labour power by employers). Lane (1991) believes that we must discover how to make the market a better agent for promoting happiness and human development (p.613) and writes of the struggle to make capitalism more efficient and more humane (p.248). Gianaris (1996:183) sees the downside for global capitalism of increasing monopoly power: '... in order to avoid the creation of exploitive and sleeping private monopolies, worldwide competition is needed.'

For every writer who wants to see more competition in markets, there is another who sees the need to restrict markets by curbing unbridled competition. The super-capitalist Soros expresses his fears for the system and his proposed remedy thus:

> Too much competition and too little cooperation can cause intolerable inequities and instability. Insofar as there is a dominant belief in our society today, it is a belief in the magic of the marketplace. The doctrine of laissez-faire capitalism holds that the common good is best served by the uninhibited pursuit of self-interest. Unless it is tempered by the recognition of a common interest that ought to take precedence over particular interests, our present system — which, however imperfect, qualifies as an open society — is liable to break down (1997:48).

Hutton, too, is very concerned about what will happen to a capitalism that allows or even encourages too much competition. He advocates reforms along the lines of unspecified countervailing powers:

> ...the operation of the unchecked market, whatever its success in sending effective messages about what is scarce and what is abundant, has an inherent tendency to produce unreasonable inequality, economic instability and immense concentrations of private, unaccountable power. To protect itself, society has to have countervailing powers built into the operation of the market, otherwise the market cannot deliver its promise. Instead it collapses into licence masquerading as liberty, spivery dressed up as risk-taking and exploitation in the guise of efficiency and flexibility (1997:4).

A very cautious approach to market reform is expressed by Hyde: '... there is little to be gained by a wholesale attack on the market. We can sometimes limit the scope of its influence, but we cannot change its nature'(1999:273). Agnew and Corbridge (1995:227) don't go beyond platitudes in recommending 'a world in which the market is at once tamed, decentralised and disestablished...'

Heilbroner is rather bolder in expressing his fears about an unregulated capitalism and more specific about the reform measures he thinks should be taken: there is no way of protecting the members of a market society from the pervasive and often dangerous side-effects of their activities except by the imposition of social controls over the market dispositions - taxes, inducements, prohibitions or regulations - and there is no source of such protective measures other than recourse to a public sector (1985:203).

A former Bishop of Durham, David Jenkins (2000:9) has greater claims to knowledge of religion than of economics, but does believe that we have the wrong kind of politics and the wrong kind of market (his capitalisation, not mine):

> ...a politics rescued from our present mind-numbing subservience to the mantra of the Market so that the Market itself can be rescued for what it is undoubtedly worth.

Make of that what you will.

Reducing inequality

A very popular way of proposing to reform capitalism is that it should reduce unacceptable inequalities between people and groups. This advocacy may be expressed in general terms, presumably to get agreement in principle for specific measures which can then follow, or directly in terms of the specific equalising reforms.

Reich (1991:301) provides an example of the first type with his statement that 'To improve the economic position of the bottom four-fifths will require that the fortunate fifth share its wealth and invest in the wealth-creating capacities of other Americans.' We may guess that the fortunate few will be more heavily taxed, pay more for their luxuries, be urged to give more to charities, and so on. When Teeple (1995:31) writes of the social democratic parties' goal of making the benefits of capitalism available to all he presumably has in mind some measures of greater equality.

There are various ways of seeking to reduce inequality while keeping the basic property system intact. This can be done both internationally and within nations, seeking to reduce the gap between rich and poor nations and between rich and poor individuals and families. Singer and Wildavsky (1993:202) believe that 'We should increase the share of our GNP we spend on helping people and countries outside the US back toward the 1 percent level we used thirty years ago...' Within the richer countries it has been proposed that big winners from gambling and lotteries should be more heavily taxed. Frank and Cook (1996:vii) actually call America the winner-take-all society and would like to see a reduction in the reward structure at the top of industries in general and the entertainment and sports industries in particular.

Some of the proposals to equalise capitalism come from those who call themselves socialists. Thus Nove (1998:221) believes that 'The level of incomes in state, socialised and co-operative enterprises should not vary greatly, to avoid social stress.' Apparently Nove accepts that incomes should remain grossly unequal in the commercial sector. Although the reduction of inequality is not specifically mentioned in Girling's advocacy of economic development as a desirable reform, it is strongly implied:

> Economic development — broadly, putting physical and human resources to productive use — may also be considered a good, by raising incomes, improving living conditions, increasing social mobility, giving access to better health, education and skills, and widening the consumer's range of choice (1987:207).

Increasing democracy

Some suggestions for reforming capitalism concern introducing or enhancing measures of democracy, broadly understood to mean greater participation by the people in the government run by their elected representatives. Such a system, sometimes touted as the people's capitalism, is thought to be superior to dictatorships, where the people are given no choice about which political party should run the system, let alone whether the system should be changed.

More democracy is advocated by those reformers who are not happy about the manifestations and direction of contemporary global capitalism, but are not willing to oppose it with anything stronger than vague platitudes. Barber (1995:279) is a good example:

> ...democracy is not someone's gift to the powerless... not a universal prescription for some singularly remarkable form of government, it is an admonition to people to live in a certain fashion: responsibly, autonomously, yet on common ground, in self-determining communities somehow still open to others, with tolerance and mutual respect yet a firm sense of their own values.

Democracy may be promoted in the political and the economic field.

Organisations such as Charter 88 in Britain seek to stimulate greater interest in voting and in standing for public office. Various measures of industrial democracy — of which workers' control is the most radical — have a long history, but relatively little success in getting workers to organise other than in unions and the occasional and usually precarious workers' co-operative. As with the reduction of inequality, proposals to increase democracy are sometimes linked with what is alleged to be socialism. Schweikart (1993:67) advocates Economic Democracy as a form of socialism featuring (among other things) worker self-management. Although, as we shall see in chapter 17, democracy is an essential feature of socialism, forms of capitalism which embody democratic elements are not thereby transformed into socialism.

Economic efficiency and welfare

One line of argument in pursuit of a better capitalism is that economic efficiency and welfare can be partners, not rivals. Mainstream economics evaluates capitalism primarily from the perspective of efficiency. While not ignoring efficiency, welfare economics discusses other criteria such as reducing inequality, increasing democracy and the building of community. Dymski and Elliott, exponents of welfare, explain its priorities thus: 'Any deficiencies associated with capitalism — poverty, inequality, insecurity, unemployment... lie in secondary domains; at least, such problems are perceived to be better accommodated once economic efficiency has been achieved'(1989:142). In other words, the primary domain is to make profits as efficiently as possible, some of which may be devoted to forms of welfare.

Welfare problems — centring around deprivations of various kinds — are felt mainly by members of the working class. Organisations representing the interests of such people within capitalism strive to improve their living standards and to share in any affluence that the system produces. Such organisations are reformist, not revolutionary. Writing of these reformist bodies, Brenner (1984:5) believes that they did not reject capitalist utilitarianism, but affirmed it, in the belief that their material needs and social interests could best be served by collective efforts in trade unions or political parties. What has been true in the past continues to be true today — if anything, so-called working class organisations are more closely integrated into the profit system than before.

Some proposals to reform capitalism are inspired by the ideas of shared ownership of capital, stakeholding and the third way (beyond free-market and state-controlled capitalism). Thus Gates (1998:xix) believes '...people are likely to become better stewards of all those systems of which they are a part — social, political, fiscal, cultural and natural — as they gain a personal stake in the economic system, with the rights and responsibilities that implies.' He looks forward to the time when more of us become connected with capitalism — as capitalists. Hutton and Giddens (2001:217) advocate an internationalist third way, blending more effective economic and social governance and social-democratic values, passionate democracy and an intense concern with human rights. In other words, the acceptable rather than the unacceptable face of capitalism, if indeed such an anatomical monstrosity can be bred.

One intriguing idea put forward as a reform of capitalism is that in certain circumstances workers should be able to hire capital. According to Bowles and Gintis (1986:74) this is not only something that should happen, it is something that does happen: in a competitive market system workers are just as capable of hiring capital (that is, obtaining loans and renting productive equipment) as capitalists are capable of hiring workers. Highly paid employees at management level do sometimes act in this way — the phenomenon is known as a management buy-out. Such changes of ownership of companies may shift the blurred line between capitalists and workers, but they do nothing to change the basis of the system. Bowles and Gintis admit as much when they say for the capitalist economy to work well workers must somehow be induced to work hard enough at low enough wages so that a surplus flows into the hands of their employer (p.211).

So far we have discussed the reforms of capitalism generated by people working together in organisations of some kind. It is also possible to advocate reforms in individual behaviour. Law-abiding, rule-conforming and morally respectable people prefer a capitalism that minimises lawlessness, rule-breaking and reprehensible behaviour. Highly commercialised capitalism may be rejected on a personal level in favour of a softer, greener and more humane form. Thus Ritzer (1993:183) advocates a number of personal reforms such as: do as many things as you can for yourself, pass up lunch at McDonald's, watch as little television as possible. Such small gestures in opposition to some features of capitalism won't change the system; they may make those who practise them feel better.

The third way/communitarianism

There has recently been a spate of talking and writing about the third way. The concept is not new. In the 1920s Mary Parker Follett (1949) was lecturing and writing about the third way of integration beyond domination and compromise. By integration she meant a creative solution which gave both parties to a dispute the essence of what they really wanted. Contemporary third way thinking is much more about the need of capitalism to avoid its excesses, usually in terms of too much market domination or state control. The same concept and practice is expressed in the advocacy of communitarianism.

British Prime Minister Tony Blair has been a keen advocate of third way politics. His academic supporter, Giddens (2000:54) explains that 'Third way social democrats should look to transform existing global institutions and support the creation of new ones... The intensifying of globalization... offers many benefits which it should be the aim of third-way politics to maximize.' In chapter 8 we shall see who are the beneficiaries of globalisation — they are certainly not the mass of people.

Communitarianism is the more American version of the third way, though both terms have been used on both sides of the Atlantic. Giddens quotes approvingly the following passage from Etzioni (1995:6): 'communitarianism represents a call to restore civic virtues and to shore up the moral foundations of society.'

Other proposed reforms

Here we look at a few more possible or actual reforms of society which more or less intentionally keep capitalism in place. I shall leave to chapter 14 discussion of reforms which are seen as seen as steps on the way to abolishing capitalism.

A reform which almost deserves to be called a revolutionary proposal is put forward by Trainer (1996:146). He advocates a conserver society instead of a consumer society, but it is still a mixed economy, with a cash sector and a communal sector: Most people would only need quite low cash incomes and would thus only need to work one day a week at a normal job in the cash sector (p.8). Some things, and perhaps many, might best be left to market forces but we would [decide] rationally which limits to put on the market... (p.147). So in the end Trainer's proposal is just another market reform, spiced with a dash of socialism.

Just to show that all capitalists aren't preoccupied with making money, Soros (1998) suggests a distinction between market behaviour and social behaviour:'...we must learn to distinguish between individual decision making as expressed in market behaviour and collective decision making as expressed in social behaviour' (p.21). This ties in with the practice of philanthropy, or its more modern equivalent, corporate citizenship. Rich people and large corporations make donations or set up charitable bodies. It is even argued that such good citizen behaviour is also good for business. It certainly is if it produces more acquiescence in the profit system.

Chapter 5

CAPITALISM, BY ITS MOSTLY CRITICAL OBSERVERS

So far we have discussed capitalism as seen through the eyes of its ardent and uncritical supporters and of those who quite like it as a basic system but think it can be improved in some way(s). Here we move to a different category who are more insistent in pointing out what is wrong with capitalism while not going quite so far as to advocate abolishing it and replacing it with something better. The next chapter will deal with the ideas of those who really want to go for fundamental change.

There is a slight risk that a few writers I have attached to one of the four viewpoints will feel they have been misallocated. Writers I quoted in chapter 3 may in fact want to see some reforms of capitalism. Chapter 4 writers may feel their proposed reforms embody quite critical observations on the contemporary system. Those in this chapter could go either way - seeing their observations as not all that critical or as serious enough to amount to outright opposition. Finally, some alleged opponents of the system may wish to downgrade their opposition to criticism. My apologies to all the above who I hope are few.

Commercialisation and consumerism

Probably the most frequent criticism made of capitalism is that it features an excess of commercialisation and consumerism. I put these two excesses together because it is difficult to separate them: they work together and are mutually reinforcing. Commercialisation is the social and economic process by which goods, services and experiences are offered for sale. Consumerism is the individual and group mindset and behaviour that is both made possible by, and is the purpose of, commercialisation.

Rifkin (2000) offers one of the most trenchant critiques available of contemporary commercialised/consumer culture. The subtitle of his book is a good summary if slight exaggeration: the new culture of hypercapitalism where all of life is a paid for experience. 'Beyond the production of goods and services for sale and profit, cultural production represents the final stage of the capitalist way of life whose essential mission has always been to bring more and more human activity into the commercial arena'(p.8). But Rifkin is not actually an opponent of the system he describes. He clearly has his preferences for, and aversions to, different types of capitalism, but he nowhere expresses any opposition to it as a system.

Heilbroner has had many critical things to say about capitalism. On the systematic commodification of life he writes 'At its core, capitalism is a social order that marshals and expends its energies in the pursuit of capital... Thus, the commodification of life is not only an intrusion of science and technology into the tissues of sociality, but also the means by which a capitalist economy draws energy from its own environment' (1995:99).

Another prolific and long time critic of capitalism, Seabrook, observes that 'the old coercive forces of poverty and want have been replaced by the near tyranny of an inscrutable and joyless community' (1974: 15).

We are a consumer generation, nurtured by advertising and salesmanship. Even our personal identity is fashioned out of elements created by others and marketed aggressively and seductively. Marketing leads frenzied consumers to hurl themselves under the wheels of debt (McQueen, 2001:326). Consumer choice, far from being free, is highly constructed (Tomlinson, 1995:5,13)

The US is without doubt the most advanced consumer society in the world — and it has the most prolific output of criticism of it. Schor points out that rich and poor alike are under pressure to consume goods and services: The poor are not so much adherents to an alternative (antimaterialist) set of values as they are unsuccessful at the same game everyone else is playing (1991:144). Far from being an unalterable trait of human nature, consumerism is itself a product of our times. Numerous examples of societies where consuming more is relatively unimportant can be found in the anthropological and historical literature.

Consumerism, like the capitalism of which it is an integral part, is by no means confined to the US and a few other economically advanced countries. Hefner (1998:9) reviews market cultures in the new Asian capitalisms and concludes that they have much in common with capitalism elsewhere: '...by making so much of our ordinary life dependent on the market, the commodification of goods and services can also render our desires and, ultimately, social identities vulnerable to manipulation by the very commercial agencies supposedly servicing our needs'.

Some consumerism is global and some relative to local conditions. Babies are offered for sale on the internet. In Japan it is possible for families without grandparents to rent them. The South Australian government has considered finding a way to make forest farmers pay for the rain that falls on their land.

In *No Logo, No Space, No Choice, No Jobs* Naomi Klein offers a devastating criticism of the dominance of brand image commodities in the First World and the conditions of ruthless exploitation which make production of such commodities possible in the Third World. She believes that something to rectify this can be done within capitalism. She is an activist who supports demonstrations, street parties and suchlike. In some mysterious way these protests are supposed to prevent the profit system from behaving in the way it has always behaved — exploiting any avenues, legal or otherwise, in search of maximum profit.

Inequalities

As we saw in chapter 3, proponents of capitalism argue that it has brought great material wealth to the world. Unfortunately, that wealth is very unequally distributed. The gap between the rich and the poor, both within countries and between countries, is getting wider. The statistics are staggering but readily available, so there is no need for me to repeat them at length here. But I will quote just a few of them for illustration:

- The world's 200 richest people own $1,000,000,000,000 while 1.3 billion people live on less than a dollar a day (Fleet and Renton, 2000:2)
- Thirty million people die of hunger every year and more than 800 million live in extreme poverty (Nielson, 2001:207)
- The 10 countries that are home to two-thirds of the world's poorest people receive only one-third of the available aid (Haywood, 1995:120)
- Between 1990 and 1999 chief executive income went from 85 times more than what average blue-collar got to around 475 times more [in the US] (Frank, 2001)
- In 1998 one in every 40 people on the planet had access to the internet; about half in the US, but one in 4,000 in Africa [excluding S. Africa] (Brown et al, 1999:94)

The doyen of free-market economics, Adam Smith, wrote that 'Wherever there is great wealth, there is great inequality. For every rich man, there must be at least 500 poor, and the affluence of the rich supposes the indigence of the many' (1986:709). The ratio of 500:1 poor to rich looks questionable even when Smith was writing at the end of the 18th century, but the point about the rich minority implying the poor majority is as true today as it ever was.

In the 1980s European sociologists feared the coming of a two-thirds society in which a third of the population (retired, unemployed or dependent on someone employed) would be impoverished. But, according to Martin and Schumann (1997), 'The new model is of a 20 to 80 world, a one-fifth society in which those left out would have to be pacified with tittytainment'(p.5). The latter is the contemporary equivalent of the Roman bread and circuses. The trend, at least in the short-to-medium term, seems inevitable. Rifkin (2000:9) foresees that 'Perhaps as little as 5 percent of the adult population will be needed to manage and operate the traditional industrial sphere by the year 2050'. The remaining 95 percent of us are presumably to be employed in the new industries which offer lived experiences for sale, or, failing employment, are to be pacified by mindless entertainment.

Frank and Cook (1996) point out that we live in an increasingly winner take all society. The reward structure common in entertainment and sports - where many aspirants compete for huge financial rewards going to a few at the top — permeates many other sectors of life. Lottery winners are paid for by the mass of relatively poor punters who live in minuscule hope of joining their number. Ironically the first winner in 1999 of the British 'Who wants to be a millionaire?' television quiz show was a woman who was far from poor.

Lip service is paid by the governments of rich countries to the principle that poor countries should be given aid. The reality is far different from the apparent intention. In 1997 official development assistance, at 0.22 percent of rich nations GDP, fell to less than half of what it was in the 1960s, even though almost all industrialised countries have committed themselves to a target of 0.7 percent (Lean, 1998:15). Developing countries are now paying rich ones more in interest on their debts than they are receiving in aid. A disproportionate amount of the aid that is received goes not to the people who need it most but to those connected with the government or the military.

Change

It is generally agreed among historians that capitalism as a system (though not as a world system) dates back to parts of Europe in the late 14th or early 15th century. However, the origins of capitalism as a relationship between capital and labour may be traced back to Flemish weavers employed by merchants in the 10th century.

From its inception capitalism has been a dynamic system, in constant change and touching — if not controlling — the lives of more and more of the world's growing population. It may be seen to have stages or types, defined in different ways by various writers. Stages imply a temporal succession of capitalist forms; types may co-exist at any given time. Silk and Silk (1996:5) outline five types or models of capitalism:

- Libertarian or laisser-faire, with a restricted role for the state
- Neoclassical, which lets the market resolve most issues within a general regulatory regime
- Mixed economy, welfare state or social market, blending government and private market decisions
- Corporate state, in which business and government work closely together
- Authoritarian or totalitarian, where a powerful government preserves the market and promotes the interests of favoured businesses

A rough temporal progression may be seen from the first of the five types to the last, with some important qualifications. Libertarian capitalism is still the political programme on which political parties of the so-called right seek power, though when in power their policies usually tend towards the centre of the mixed economy. Forms of authoritarian capitalism have been defeated in war or by more economically effective market forces, although some still survive in parts of the Third World. Corporate state capitalism is the dominant type in the early 2lst century, and promises to be so for some time to come.

The motor of change within capitalism of any type is technological change, enabling increased productivity and resulting in the death or decline of old industries and the birth or development of new ones. The decline of the welfare state has meant the end of the principle — never attained by more than a small fraction of the world's workforce — of a job for life. The reserve army of the unemployed has grown. Several hundred million peasants in Latin America and Asia are becoming proletarians, exchanging a precarious living on the land for the lowest wages that employers can get away with paying.

Compared with a century or so ago, capitalism is now stronger than ever. It increasingly permeates our lives and our world. Challenges to it for the most part amount to no more than proposing, and sometimes achieving, changes in one form of the beast to another.

In its early days the capitalist market had fewer things to sell to the general population, so it encroached relatively little on their lives. Progress for the profit system has meant expanding markets, converting public commons to private enclosures, buying and selling goods, services and experiences that were formerly made and enjoyed by the community and its members. Laclau and Mouffe describe the far-reaching change that has taken place: 'Today it is not only as a seller of labour-power that the individual is subordinated to capital, but also through his or her incorporation into a multitude of other social relations: culture, free-time, education, sex and even death. There is practically no domain of individual or collective life which escapes capitalist relations' (1985:161)

Particular administrations of capitalism are frequently — and in democracies routinely — challenged by alternative would-be leaders. The system itself is not challenged, except by a tiny minority of socialists who are presently too few to even afford the cost of putting up candidates at elections. So the US election of 2000 and the British election of 2001 were largely fought between two personalities, between two political programmes that differed only marginally. Before the British election of 1997, Pilger, a ferocious critic of capitalism but who nowhere calls for its replacement, observed 'In its quest to out-Tory the Tories, Labour has become the New Right in what is, in effect, a one-party state' (1994:114).

Turner, unlike Pilger a sociologist rather than a journalist, comes to a similar conclusion: '...there is little or no evidence, at the level of the street as it were, that the dominance of industrial capitalism as a system has been in any sense at all challenged by working-class political movements in the 1970s and 1980s (1986:230). The same may be said about the 1990s and looks like being repeated in the 2000s. It is a manifestation of hegemony, a process in which workers are persuaded to co-operate with, or at least acquiesce in, the system that exploits them. We shall return to this subject in chapter 9.

The class struggle lives on

Defenders of capitalism downplay, or even deny, the existence of classes in society. Critics, usually but not always following Marx, maintain that classes are an inescapable feature of the present system. Moreover, one class, the subordinate working class, is always on the losing side as far as material prosperity is concerned. The other class, the one that owns the lion's share of the means of wealth production and distribution, is always a winner, despite any ups and downs of its individual members. The capitalist system of classes of classes is about control of wealth, antagonism of interest, and the preservation of an elite. Greider looks at the system over its lifetime and stresses the process of control:

> The fundamental struggle, then as now, is between capital and labour. That struggle is always about control of the workplace and how the returns of the enterprise shall be divided. In both dimensions capital is winning big again, claiming a steadily larger share of returns and asserting greater control over employees, just as it did in Marx's time (1997:39).

Other critics focus their analysis of class struggle on its antagonistic nature. Thus Holloway: 'The core of capitalism (as of other class societies) is antagonistic, the daily repeated struggle by the dominant class to pump surplus labour out of the direct producers. That is the class struggle: grinding, everyday, so unspectacular that it is not even seen by bourgeois theory' (1991:171). This is a little overstated. Much is done by modern capitalism to reduce the amount of grinding experienced by the working class. More importantly, the class struggle is invisible, not just to bourgeois theory, but is made invisible to the vast mass of workers themselves

Then there is the elite-mass dimension of class struggle. Scott is able to assure us that 'A capitalist class of propertied families owing their superior life-chances to the income and wealth that is generated by their possession and use of property can still be found at the head of the stratification system of contemporary industrial capitalism' (1997:312). So no fear of trickle-down impoverishing the few at the top.

Finally, there has to be some explanation of why the exploited mass are, broadly speaking, content to be taken for mugs. One answer lies in what Dugger calls enabling myths:

> Numerous and powerful enabling myths make the underlying population's true situation unclear to its members and enable the leisure class to continue its dominant position... Enabling myths create scapegoats and protect leisure class interest against popular discontent... enabling myths encourage thinking in terms of industrious people versus lazy welfare cheats, humble white folks against arrogant black ones... (2000:38).

For reasons which need not be spelled out here, I doubt whether leisure class is the most apt description of capitalists. Ironically, the profit system affords little leisure to some of its more industrious beneficiaries, while free time (the poor person's substitute for real leisure) is the lot of many of the unemployed.

Competition is destructive

There is no harm, and sometimes much fun, in people competing to see who can run the fastest or give the most correct answers in a quiz. But it's a different matter when people are forced to compete for food, housing, health services, and jobs in a world that has enough food to feed everyone and enough labour and know-how to meet all reasonable human needs. The profit system decrees that the winners are those who are well supplied with money to buy what they need. The losers are not.

We live in a highly competitive and individualistic society, and the pressures on us to strive, to achieve, to 'get ahead' are enormous (Wachtel, 1983:47). When everyone else is racing to get ahead, not to do so is to fall behind. Yet it is demeaning and ultimately destructive of the social fabric to be obliged to organise our daily activities so centrally around the idea of trying to get the better of others. Competition is seen to be good, and co-operation devalued. Competition is alleged to be 'human nature', but Kohn (1990) is able to show that co-operation is in fact 'the brighter side of human nature'.

Most critics of capitalism are concerned not so much with the competitive basis of the profit system as with the fact that quite often this competition is unfair. As Kohn (1986:70) observes, it is a curious race indeed in which one competitor must try to scramble up from poverty while another starts out with a huge trust fund. People learn to divide themselves into winners and losers and to blame themselves for being among the losers if that is where they end up. No one stands to benefit more from a non-competitive society than those who have been cheated by a competitive one.

Chapter 6

CAPITALISM, BY ITS REVOLUTIONARY OPPONENTS

The writers whose views on capitalism we shall consider here differ substantially from those in the three previous chapters. They don't support the profit system, they are not concerned with promoting reforms of it, and their basic criticisms of it lead them to reject all forms of it. They are not necessarily opposed to particular reforms of the system (such as having 'democratic' rather than 'totalitarian' administrations of it) but they are opposed to policies of reformism, which they believe divert attention from the need to change the system fundamentally.

Because revolutionary opponents of capitalism are at present few in number and often lack adequate research and publicity resources, they rely heavily on the critical writings of those whose work we considered in the previous chapter. But they go further: the point, as they see it, is not merely to understand the system, but to work to change it. The revolutionary approach is essentially a comprehensive approach: criticism, levelled at one part of the system, can be shown to link up with criticism of other parts, ultimately of the whole. Of course it is not possible to talk about every facet of the whole at the same time, but all discussion of detail is linked, potentially if not actually, with discussion of the big picture.

Somewhat arbitrarily, I divide the authors whose work is to be considered in this chapter into two groups of avowed and academic revolutionaries. The first and smaller group identify themselves as revolutionary socialists (they may be, or have been, academics, but that is not primarily how they choose to present themselves). The second group, the academics, make statements and pursue arguments which contribute to revolutionary socialism, but they tend to be less overtly committed to the public declaration of their revolutionary ideas. I know how at least some of them feel, because in seeking employment I have been in that position myself.

Avowed revolutionaries

In their book *State Capitalism: the Wage System Under New Management* (1986) Buick and Crump argue that, whether capitalism is free market or state, it is still basically the same system. They define capitalism as having six essential characteristics:

- commodity production, most wealth being produced for sale on a market
- capital invested in production with a view to profit
- exploitation of wage and salary labour
- regulation of production for the market via a competitive struggle
- capital accumulation out of profits
- a single world economy

State capitalism existed in the USSR and elsewhere at the time Buick and Crump were writing, but has now largely given way to the free market form. It differed marginally but not fundamentally from free market capitalism. It featured state ownership of the principal means of production, the market for which was monitored and directed by state functionaries, and a planned economy. Whether capitalism is predominantly free market or state, workers are obliged to sell their labour power as a commodity, hence losing control over its use to the employing organisation, state or private. Political regimes which embraced state capitalism were defeated, not because they were 'socialist', but because they ran the market system less successfully than their free market/mixed economy rivals (see chapter 7).

Perrin (2000) concentrates his analysis of capitalism on two major themes: its tendency to alternate between booms and slumps and its resilience in face of repeated predictions of its collapse. He sums up his attitude to these issues as follows: 'Worse and more frequent crises, yes, more unemployment, yes, a great worsening of conditions for the working class, yes, but collapse — no' (p.96). Perrin's book is essentially a history of the Socialist Party of Great Britain. He traces both the ups and downs of capitalism in the 20th century and the SPGB's evaluation of those events. For example, there was in the 1950s and 60s a widespread belief among orthodox economists that the days of uncontrollable mass unemployment were over. This was soon proved wrong.

On the related issue of the resilience of the profit system Perrin quotes various views expressed from the 1880s onwards that capitalism was about to collapse. In particular there was a persistent belief that it would suffer a crisis of over-production, caused by the inability of the workers and capitalists combined to buy back the entire social product. This belief also proved to be wrong. In Perrin's view, 'capitalism will drag on endlessly until the working class consciously put an end to it' (p.96).

Ken Smith has written two books opposing capitalism. In the first (1988) he draws attention to the main defects of what he prefers to call the market system rather than capitalism. These include its enormous waste, its callousness, its enforced idleness, immense divisiveness and destructiveness. He illustrates all this by various industries run for profit, notably the food for the mind industry (manufacturing public opinion), the disease industry (treating symptoms not causes), and the money industry (making money not things).

In his second book (1994) Smith develops some of the themes raised in the first. Among these are environmental degradation, unemployment, revolution not reformism, and stultifying 'materialism' (this last refers to the argument about whether materialism denies humankind free will). Perhaps Smith's most important insight is that in politics obedience and support are the same:

> No government can survive in the developed world without the co-operation of its subjects. Recalcitrant minorities can be dealt with. But if most of the people cease active participation, the regime crumbles and no tanks or machine guns can make them. (p.25)

Stratman (n.d.), like Smith, is a somewhat wayward anti-capitalist. Much of his book expresses mainstream objections to capitalism plus advocating replacing it with something fundamentally different (he calls this 'revolutionary democracy'). For Stratman capitalism is not merely an economic system, 'It is a system of human relations, which projects and enforces its own view of the world as its primary source of control' (p.3). However, he believes that Marx's theory contains a fatal contradiction: 'his view of workers as dehumanised is inconsistent with the idea of workers fighting for revolution as conscious historical subjects' (p.164). My own view, while having some sympathy for the claim that Marx was too preoccupied with the economics of capitalism rather than helping to build socialism, is that converting people from passive acquiescence in capitalism to active opposition to it, while difficult, is not impossible.

Craig (1997) is clear that such an alternative world to capitalism must be a world without money, nation states, war and politicians. His book contains a wealth of statistics about the inequalities, deprivation and misery caused by the profit system. Unfortunately his proposed remedy falls far short of what is required. It amounts to a single voice crying out on a single issue: '... world-wide DEMANDS for the total destruction, and permanent abolition, of weapons of any size and type on or before 1st January 2001'. Admirable in itself, that demand was not met because it was aimed at one of the symptoms of capitalism and not at the disease itself, and because it was expressed by one individual and not by an organised social movement.

Academic revolutionaries

These are people whose focus is on what their work within an academic field can imply for supporting the change from capitalism to another system that they may or may not call socialism. In some cases — such as Greider and Wachtel — I have quoted them in the previous chapter as critics of the profit system. Here I quote them further to show how criticism which is often brushed aside may extend to opposition which is more damaging to the existing system and more creative in respect of the new.

Bonefeld and Holloway (1995) are lecturers in politics in the University of Edinburgh. In the introductory chapter to the book they edited they make it clear that for them money is 'a form of social relations, a form of class struggle'. They conclude:

> Our hope is that this book will contribute in a small way to the construction of a reasonable society in which humanity exists as a purpose rather than as a resource for the accumulation of money. The critique of capitalist exploitation entails a critique of 'money' and the understanding that the liberation from exploitation means a liberation from money (p.6).

Burgmann (1985, 1993) is a historian specialising in the study of the Australian labor movement and new social movements. In her 1985 book Burgmann shows how, in the period 1885–1905, there was huge and unjustified optimism about the coming of 'socialism'. In the later book she concentrates her fire on the multiplicity of new social movements — for feminism, peace, the environment, and so on — which pose a myriad of reformist alternatives to the present social order rather than a single revolutionary one. Her earlier book concludes:

> Empirically, reformist strategies for socialism can be seen to have failed.

> Revolutionaries were likewise frustrated in their anticipation that they would see socialism in their time: too many socialists were reformists, enamoured in the main of parliamentary strategies, for a mass revolutionary movement to develop. However, revolutionary strategies, unlike reformist strategies, cannot be said to have failed in their application (p.198).

Pepper (1993) is a geographer, an ecologist, and a socialist. His book *Eco-socialism* has the sub-title 'from deep ecology to social justice '. He identifies as both a red and a green, which means he is broadly in support of what he calls the red-green project. The aspect of capitalism with which he is most concerned is its adverse effect on the environment — he quotes Marx extensively and approvingly on this. In defining eco-socialism Pepper is clear that 'Production will not be built on wage-slavery, but on volunteered labour, which most people will want to give to fulfil themselves and relate to others' (p.234). However, I think he is rather too keen to narrow red-green differences — in doing so he makes some incredibly sweeping generalisations, for example that red is for modernism and is absolute (p.244).

In a provocatively titled article 'Virtual capitalism', Dawson and Foster (1998) show how a critical approach to communication within capitalism can and should extend to a revolutionary approach to the system itself: 'The critique of existing communications must reach beyond a shallow critique of commercialization and extend to monopoly capital and the global system itself. Above all, it must be realized that nothing can be won, nothing of any value saved, except by opposing the system itself (p.64) .

As a magazine editor, Greider (1997) may not strictly qualify as an academic, but his several previous radical books justify his inclusion here. In *One World, Ready or Not* Greider contends that the global economy is sowing 'creative destruction' everywhere, making possible great accumulations of wealth while reviving forms of human exploitation that characterised industry a hundred years ago:

> Revolution offers the opportunity to rethink the largest questions and, in fact, compels people to reexamine what they have always taken for granted (p.44).

Kolko (1988) is another author whose literary output justifies her inclusion as an academic revolutionary. It is only slightly unfortunate that she chooses the essentially capitalist term 'economy' to describe the world she wishes to change. Kolko is very clear that the state everywhere acts as the promoter of profit and the antagonist of labour. Her view of the need for revolution, not reform, is equally plain:

> Socialism is not capitalism by another name, nor 'capitalism with a human face', but the negation of capitalism — that is, of its systemic features, its' laws — and the affirmation and construction of a different system altogether. ...And socialism can exist only when the systemic features of capitalism no longer define society (p.351).

Marquand (1997) has a background of publications in economics, politics and sociology. Earlier, he notes, there was a public domain, ring-fenced from the pressures of the market place, in which citizenship rights rather than market power governed the allocation of social goods. Now privatisation, overt or disguised, is narrowing the scope of this public domain. However,

> nothing has happened to invalidate the socialist ethic. The values of community and fellowship speak as loudly (or, of course, as faintly) to the late 20th century as to earlier periods. Indeed, in some respects they are more pertinent (p.68).

Wachtel (1983) is a psychologist and journalist. His book *The Poverty of Affluence* is addressed to an American audience ready for radicalism if not for revolution. He asks: how is it that the very thinking that produces our wealth keeps us from enjoying what we have? Where have we gone wrong? What is to be done? Respectively, his answers are that our materialistic preoccupations actually diminish our security and enjoyment of life. We went wrong because of our 'isolating individualism' . And 'I do think that some shift in the direction of communal ownership will have to occur, as well as a rather substantial turn away from the profit motive as the main guiding force in the economy and in the decisions of responsible individuals... If institutional changes are required to unbind us from the wheel of wanting and buying and wanting some more, those can come from the will of the people, with votes and arguments the mechanism, not guns and dictates' (pp.146, 292)

Finally Worster (1988) specialises in what he calls the new and rapidly growing field of environmental history. His chapter 'The vulnerable earth: toward a planetary history' does not discuss socialism or communism as a possible future, but what he says about capitalism and its future replacement entitles him to be considered as at least an honorary revolutionary:

> The capitalists and their theoreticians promised that through the technological domination of the earth they could deliver a more fair, rational, efficient, and productive life for everyone, themselves above all. Their method was simply to free individual enterprise from the bonds of traditional hierarchy and

community, whether the bonding derived from other humans or the environment. That meant teaching everyone to treat the earth, as well as each other, with a frank, energetic self-assertiveness, unembarrassed by too many moral or aesthetic sentiments. To behave otherwise must be tantamount to failure as a human being. People must begin to work and produce not for the purpose of meeting their own family and community needs directly, but for selling to others, more often than not to strangers... No cultural drive has lasted forever, unchanged, unchallenged, unchastened. It may be that this one is beginning to wear off at last (pp.11, 20).

Chapter 7

FREE MARKET OR STATE CONTROL?

Capitalism, in various countries and at various times, may be divided into two major forms. The usual labels for these forms are free-market or state-controlled. The first form is often identified with democracy, and the second with 'communism'. Both terms need the inverted commas. Some countries whose economies are primarily free-market are political dictatorships: the market may be free to enter — if you have the necessary cash — but the people are not free; they are unable to choose their rulers, much less to change the system under which they live. The so-called communist countries do not —perhaps I should say did not — embrace communism as an alternative to capitalism; they simply had an economy which featured a relatively high degree of state control and centralised planning.

In the two sections of this chapter I have two related aims. The first is to show that what in some quarters is called 'actually existing socialism' (Burbach et al, 1997:153) was and is no such thing, being a state-controlled form of capitalism. My second aim is to argue that 'free' market is not really free: all markets are subject to a degree of control, whether by the state or other forces designed to ensure that the profit system operates efficiently and in the interest of possessors and controllers of capital.

Actually existing state capitalism

There was certainly a revolution in Russia in 1917, but it was not a revolution which changed the capitalist basis of Russian society. The country had a small industrial capacity, a small working class, and the greatest part of the peasantry was illiterate (Lane, 1970:50). The Bolshevik party, under the leadership of Lenin, was able to seize power from the Tsarist autocracy because it offered a programme of confiscation of all landlords' estates, the establishment of a single national bank, and control of production by a government made up of the Soviets of Workers' Deputies.

Writing well before the overthrow of the rule of the Communist Party in

1989, Hollander (1973:378) described some of the similarities between Soviet and American society. Both countries had social problems such as crime, juvenile delinquency and family instability. Both mismanaged natural resources and failed to eradicate various kinds of pollution. Both had systems of stratification based on educational and occupational achievement. Both were military superpowers, spending a large proportion of their budgets on preparing for war. One 'difference' noted by Hollander has proved correct but in the wrong direction. He thought that 'The Soviet Union is justly perceived as stable' and that most Soviet citizens probably find the type of stability attained relatively satisfying'. The change from Soviet state capitalism to Russian free market (and black market) capitalism has proved 'satisfying' only to a few who, as in capitalism elsewhere, are able to exploit others.

The 1989 change of regime in Russia is sometimes described as a staging post in the process of reform. I prefer the view that what happened was the replacement of the old central command system with state-capitalist networks in which enrichment of small groups is the main aim. The battle between free market and state controlled forms of capitalism has apparently been decisively won by the former. To socialists, who had all along denied that the 1917 revolution had ushered in a period of socialism, the defeat came as no surprise and no great disappointment. But it did serve to dash the hopes of those who falsely believed that capitalism had been replaced by 'actually existing socialism' .The opponents of socialism were among those most insistent that what had been defeated was socialism: 'it has been tried and it has failed', with the implication that it would be a waste of time and effort to try again.

According to Heilbroner (1995:80) 'the collapse of the Soviet system changed the view of capitalism from a mixture of enthusiasm and trepidation to a kind of acquiescence in its unchallenged hegemony... with regard to economic expansion... there was no longer a credible alternative to which to turn.' By having offered state capitalism - under the guise of 'socialism' — as a credible alternative to free market capitalism, the supporters of the Soviet regime did a great disservice to the cause of socialism. That disservice is matched only by the efforts of social democrats — again, at least initially, under the guise of 'socialism' — to administer a 'better' capitalism. The result is that today almost everyone is persuaded that the only question to resolve is: what kind of capitalism can we support?

Not which but how much of each

There is an old socialist saying that, when you are faced with the choice of the lesser of two evils, you should choose neither .The choice between free market capitalism and state capitalism is a good example. In fact the choice - perhaps it would be better to say policy preference — between the one and the other is not simple and clear-cut. All forms of 'free market' capitalism involve some role for the state. And all forms of state capitalism feature markets in some spheres of economic activity which are relatively free from control by the state.

Plant (1985:3) believes there are only two approaches to understanding the nature of contemporary society:

> One approach is based on the allocation of economic resources through the decision mechanism run by a central government bureaucracy and according to the preferences of central government bureaucrats. This approach is called socialism. The other system of solving society's fundamental economic problem is based on not allocating resources by a central government bureaucracy. This system is called capitalism. There are only two protocols to choose from, although all modern societies combine some elements of both.

The 'approach' that Plant calls socialism is clearly intended to refer to state capitalism as evident in the Soviet regime. He conveniently overlooks the fact that that regime featured markets. If he were writing today he would see even more clearly that markets feature in the post-Soviet regime. However, it is to his credit that he sees all modem societies as combining elements of both free and state controlled markets.

Another unacceptable claim is that there is a socialist economy within capitalism. Green and Sutcliffe (1987:373) put it thus:

> ...nationalized industries, workers' co-operatives, workers' control, aspects of the welfare state, adult education opportunities, progressive income tax, technical progress which removes drudgery, economic assistance to underdeveloped countries, positive discrimination or affirmative action in favour of women or blacks, are all partial or distorted but actually existing elements of a socialist economy within capitalism.

Green and Sutcliffe, whose book is titled *The Profit System: the Economics of Capitalism* are no friends of socialism, but they do the profit system an injustice by locating such measures as nationalised industries, adult education and overseas aid as outside that system. All of the measures they list (with the possible exception of workers' control, which they almost certainly don't mean literally) are compatible with capitalism and make that system more acceptable and thus able to run better.

Rueschemeyer and Evans (1985:48) use the term 'pacts of domination' to describe the co-operation between leaders in industry and government (reminding us of Wright Mills' (1956) identification of a circulating power elite of economic, political and military personnel) and they note the contradictory features in the presentation of the state's functions:

> ...the state tends to be an expression of pacts of domination, to act coherently as a corporate unit, to become an arena of social conflict, and to present itself as the guardian of universal interests.

There are persistent attempts to simplify complex reality, to see a small number of woods rather than a confusingly large number of trees. Albert (1993) makes such an attempt with his three ages of capitalism:

- from 1791, capitalism against the state
- from 1891, capitalism disciplined by the state
- from 1991, capitalism instead of the state

This categorisation is not without value, but in many ways it is a gross over-simplification. In the first period the market was given relatively free rein, mainly because support for state intervention was weak. In the second period it was recognised that the state could be a great help to the market system by controlling its worst excesses, though 'disciplined', which implies all stick and no carrot, hardly seems the right term. The third period, which we have only recently entered, is one in which capitalism, in the form of multinational corporations, has supposedly taken over most, if not all, state functions. Such reports of the death of the state are much exaggerated.

Another way of categorising capitalisms is by what function the state plays in administering them. Coates (2000:19) distinguishes four such types:

- state activity to strengthen markets/correct market failures
- the state to engage in economic management
- the state to create market advantage for selected enterprises (subsidy/tax advantage)
- state regulation and control of economic processes

The first is the neoliberal (Thatcherite or Reaganite) policy of a minimal, but nevertheless essential, role for the state. The second is the Keynesian or public works approach to try to minimise booms and slumps. The third is when the state injects money into enterprises that private capital regards as unattractive, for example certain transport routes, Concorde, the London Dome. The fourth is exemplified by the former capitalisms of Eastern Europe. Perhaps we should add a fifth: the nation state as supplicant to multinational corporations (a subject to which we shall return in the next chapter).

Sometimes the state is equated with the public sector, in apparent opposition to the private sector of the (free) market. The truth is that a completely uncontrolled market is a dangerous thing, even to those who support the idea most enthusiastically.

However that does not mean that the public sector is immune from commercial considerations. Offe (1984:263) is wrong to believe that 'welfare' interests are a pre-condition of the commodification of labour power. Just as slavery was abolished not because it was inhuman but because it was inefficient, so capitalism introduced 'welfare' in order to exploit labour more efficiently.

There is an impressive list of the ways in which the state (public sector) functions to smooth the path and solve the problems of the 'free' market. The list includes legislation to counter the extremes of the business cycle, to provide unprofitable but essential economic services, to defend and promote the interests of national capital in domestic and overseas markets, to ensure the reproduction of the working class, to act as guarantor of social order, to mitigate working-class interest in revolutionary change, and so on (Teeple, 1995:26). Public education and the various 'benefits' offered by the welfare state may be added to the list. It is almost as if capital, in failing to subdue the unruly pressures of money and labour, invited the state to move in and take over (Hodgson, 1982:230).

In summing up both the false claims of state capitalism to be socialist and the equally false supposition that the state operates against the market rather than providing it with a favourable environment, I can do no better than to quote Wood (1995:289):

> The old choice between the market and centralized planning is barren. Both in their various ways have been driven by the imperatives of accumulation — in one case imposed by the demands of competition and profit maximization internal to the system, in the other by the requirements of accelerated

industrial development. Neither has involved the reappropriation of the means of production by the producers, neither has been motivated by the interests of the workers whose surplus labour is appropriated, nor indeed by the interests of the people as a whole.

Chapter 8

GLOBALISATION, NATION STATES AND THE NEW TECHNOLOGY

Globalisation was a buzzword in the 1990s and it looks like continuing well into the new century. It sums up a number of significant changes within the world capitalist system. These changes affect every sphere of life and society, and they are based on technological developments, particularly in information and communication. But is globalisation really something new - or have the claims for its novelty and its consequences been overstated? The new technology has changed both the material and non-material environment of people in the First World and is promising (or threatening?) to do the same in the Third World. But is this the direction in which we should be seeking to go? Have political nation states become victims of economic globalisation, or are they its willing and needed partners? These are the main questions to be posed and hopefully answered in this chapter.

Yes, we are all being globalised

As with attitudes to capitalism itself, attitudes to globalisation tend to fall into different groups. There are those who embrace the idea and the practice warmly, those who are not against it but would like to reform it, those who on the whole are critical of it, and others who definitely oppose it. However, those four groups don't exactly correspond with the views on capitalism which we considered in chapters 3–6. Socialists see socialism as a potential world society and therefore in a sense they support the principle of globalisation. And being an opponent of globalisation — for instance because you see it as destroying traditional national cultures — doesn't necessarily mean you are an opponent of capitalism.

Globalisation means that many goods and services and experiences marketed under specific brand names are increasingly available in different countries around the world. The evidence is not hard to find — directly if you travel internationally and indirectly in the media if you don't. CNN is the global television. Coke is the global drink. Macs are the global fast-food (Suter, 1995:74). The duty-free airport shops, the most placeless of all places, offer the same Pentax cameras, Sony Walkmen, Chivas Regal whisky or Suchard chocolate (Sampson, 1989: 142). Not necessarily branded but well advertised pizzas, croissants and sushi are spreading around the world. A London advertising agency announced the good news that the consumer now has a 'global relationship' with advertising.

One notable feature of the global economy is that it favours intangible things — ideas, information and relationships, which are interlocked. The world of computers, entertainment and telecommunications is now collectively a larger industry than any of the old giants such as construction, food products or car manufacturing (Kelly, 1998:3). 'Integrated marketing' now permeates much of what we see and read and listen to (Pilger, 1998:69). Disney has a 'tie-in' with McDonald's, Warner Bros with Burger King. The Olympic Games are virtually owned by Coca-Cola, Nike, Reebok, the oil companies and the other conglomerates which pay for multi-million-dollar 'endorsements'. Multi-media Murdoch controls much of the rest.

The politician John Redwood (1993), nicknamed Vulcan because of his somewhat unearthly demeanour, is a keen advocate of globalisation. Writing on behalf of the business community, Redwood asserts that the United Kingdom 'has made it clear that it recognizes the growing tendency towards global business and wants to be part of that process' (p.15). He also equates globalisation with 'popular capitalism' and makes the sinister prediction that 'The politicians who try to resist it will be tossed aside like trees in a hurricane' (p.145).

Catley (1996) has a different view of how globalisation is impinging on Australian capitalism. He sees that country as having abandoned a 'hybrid system of economic regulation' that 'combined capitalist rhetoric with strong state intervention' (p.213). Catley believes that Australian capitalism is now fully committed to the process of globalisation, 'making it inherently competitive, internally market-driven, externally in balance with the world economy and institutionally oriented to efficiency'. In other words it is, like all the other capitalisms, competing for world markets.

Finally, Nelson Mandela (1996) sees globalisation as something in which he would like South Africa to participate more fully. He divides the countries of the world into three groups: rich, poor and others like his own in the middle:

> Today the rich countries are living in a glorious pool of permanent economic light. Beyond this rim of light, a secondary group of countries is found; it lives in a kind of economic dusk. Further away — beyond the pool of light and shade — the greater number of countries and peoples of the world live in an economic darkness... Full participation in the global trading system is central to securing South Africa's international economic relations. For the sake of our democracy, we need to be in the pool of light (p.294).

Allowing that Mandela is a decent man who would like every human being on the planet to be in the 'pool of light', this just isn't a realisable aim. The power elites in the rich countries are in control of the electricity generating plant. The analogy breaks down because 'the glorious pool of permanent economic light' is neither permanent nor enjoyed by large minorities, of the population even in the 'rich' countries. Equal access to *light*, not to a *pool* of light, is a desirable and realisable aim.

No, we're not, it's nothing new

Those who claim that globalisation is both relatively new and pervasive are opposed by two groups. One group doesn't deny that there is such a thing as globalisation but believes that, rather than being new, it is a process that has been going on within capitalism for some time. The other group attacks the proposition that globalisation means the domination of multinational corporations over nation states. The arguments of the two groups are to some extent mutually reinforcing but need to be considered separately.

Sampson (1989:143) argues that there is nothing new about rich people displaying their wealth in clothes and ornaments bought in global markets. It happened in ancient Arab countries and in medieval Europe. But the late 20th century developed a new kind of portable wealth, the carrying not of gold and jewels but expensive fantasies and brand names announcing that the purchaser belonged to a certain social class. Bryan and Farrell (1996:168) argue that the process of globalisation has been under way for centuries. Global capitalism merely accelerates the process of creating a dynamic, diverse world market for goods and services.

Perhaps the best example of the long-term development, rather than the recent novelty, of globalisation is the invention of the telegraph — what Standage (1998) calls the Victorian internet. He describes how, during Queen Victoria's reign, a new technology was developed that allowed people to communicate almost instantly across great distances, shrinking the world faster and further than ever before. It revolutionised business practice, gave rise to new forms of crime, and inundated its users with a deluge of information. The hopes and fears associated today with the internet are mirrored by those inspired by the telegraph. Standage suggests that if any generation has the right to claim that it bore the full bewildering, world-shrinking brunt of such revolution it is not us — it is our 19th century forebears (p.199).

Another critical view of globalisation as a process of multinationals gaining dominance over nation states is to offer an alternative interpretation of what is taking place. Rather than being rivals, corporations and governments are seen to work as partners in the profit-seeking enterprise. Global capitalism gets support and services from governments in several different ways:

- funding of education and research
- providing tax incentives for research and development
- public contracts to protect internal markets
- providing support and assistance, e.g. regulatory, diplomatic and political

Weiss (1998) is right to debunk what he calls the myth of the powerless state. If anything, globalisation makes the state more salient. Just because some multinational corporations have budgets that exceed those of some Third World nation states does not mean that all nation states are relatively powerless. Governments still have, if not a monopoly, at least a predominance of force within their own boundaries (Jay, 2000:332). Without the participation of the state, transnational capital could not keep its indispensable markets open and its boundaries closed. Nor could it manipulate the price of labour power and raw materials. Capitalism is impossible without laws, and laws do not exist outside states (Kagarlitsky, 2000:17). So it is reasonable to agree with Wood (1998:12) that the nation state, rather than having been weakened by globalisation, is its main agent.

Who gains from globalisation?

The globalised media spend vast sums of money to tell us that what they have to offer is good for us — if we can afford to pay for it. There are, of course, advantages for the entrepreneurial globalisers: removal of or reduction in trade barriers, cheaper bulk transport costs, cheaper long-distance communications, reduction or abolition of foreign exchange controls (Northcott, 1991:13). Having no particular reason for preferring one country to another, multinational corporations shift production, sales, R and D, investment funds, personnel between different locations with a view to minimising costs and maximising growth, productivity and profit.

Governments in Third World countries, on behalf of their own power elites, do all they can to invite multinational corporations to take up profit-seeking residence. Those governments offer cost-reducing concessions — lower taxes, low-cost utilities, and low-cost 'docile' semi-skilled or unskilled labour (Carnoy, 1993:62). In the most poverty-stricken areas of the Third World it may be argued that low wages are better than no wages. But in many parts of the developing world this doubtful 'advantage' does not apply. The global free market has resulted in over 100 million peasants becoming migrant labourers in China (Gray, 1998:3). In Europe and elsewhere tens of millions of workers have become unemployed, many for long periods and with little or no unemployment pay.

There is no doubt that globalisation has increased the gap between rich and poor countries and between rich and poor people. Problems within the global capitalist system are generally solved by benefiting the owners of capital rather than the non-owners (workers). Sherman (2000:46) gives the example of new channels for high-resolution television being given to the owners of the present channels.

New technology — blessing or curse?

Recent developments in various forms of technology (collectively called the new technology) have helped the process of globalisation. They have also had effects on the quality of life of producers and consumers. In what respects, if any, has the new technology represented human progress? Has it helped to make capitalism more acceptable and secure, or does it have the potential to play a part in replacing that system by socialism?

First, the blessings. Technology has come a long way in my lifetime. When I was born in 1927 radio was in its infancy, there was no television, long-distance travel was for an adventurous and wealthy minority, and the idea of the computer as we know it today would have seemed truly fantastic. The diagnosis and treatment of disease has been greatly improved by medical technology. We can buy exotic food transported from the other side of the world. Many people do not regard their mobile phone as a luxury — they see it as a necessity. The optimists believe that the internet, access to which has spread rapidly in the last few years, will make it possible for people to group together and organise in the future (Hiebert and Gibbons, 2000:316).

In these and numerous other ways technology has added to the material possessions, available services and experiences, and complexity of the lives of many people in the First World and elites in the Third World. There is the possibility of new technology bringing its wares into the lives of increasing numbers of people in developing and Third World countries. This prospect is heavily promoted by the global media as good, if not inescapable.

But other voices are not so sanguine about the advantages that the new technology has brought and can bring. The computer, in particular, is the target for critical evaluation of what it is doing to people and society. Television, video games, computers put the world at a distance from ourselves — we experience everything at one or more removes. Talbott (1995:356–60) spells this out:

> The computer is the embodiment of all those aspects of our thinking that are automatic, deterministic, algorithmic — all those aspects that can, on the strength of the past, run by themselves, without any need for conscious *presence*... What we embed in the computer is the inert and empty shadow, or abstract reflection, of the past operation of our own intelligence (author's emphasis).

What does it mean to confront today's computerised technology as a human being? We find ourselves locked in an intimate liaison with our machines, and with the machine-like tendencies in ourselves. We are invited into a world of programmed responses and of data-base-receptacles, collecting and seeking to organise and re-format mountains of information. But we do so within the parameters of the past and present. Deceptively promising to exercise our imagination, the computer in practice does nothing to help us transform ourselves. It limits our freedom to act out of the future rather than the past.

There is a wider point to be made about the new technology which includes what the use of computers is doing to ourselves and our society but goes further. It is important to understand that technology is not neutral, composed of tools that can be used for good or evil depending on the user. Technology comes bearing the purposes and values of the system that spawns it. Sale (1995:266) explains: 'Since technology is, by its very essence, artificial —

that is to say, not natural, a human construct not otherwise found in nature, where there is no technology — it tends to distance humans from their environment and set them in opposition to it.'

Virtual reality (VR) is one of technology's newest toys. VR is 'an advanced form of three-dimensional computer graphical simulation in which a participant is plunged into an artificial multimedia environment' (Coveney and Highfield, 1995:433). VR is about simulation, a concept much discussed among postmodernists, who see a world increasingly dominated by signs and symbols and make-believe. Advertisers have long known that you don't sell women shoes, you sell them pretty feet. You don't just sell a man a car, you sell him an image of what kind of man he is or would like to be. VR goes a step further; you sell people an 'experience' of part of the world without actually being there.

Rheingold (1991) is both an enthusiast and a critic of VR. He believes we are on the brink of having the power to create any (virtual) experience we desire:

> We might decide that we wouldn't mind becoming a little or a lot more machinelike in exchange for labour-saving devices, life-saving tools, attractive conveniences and seductive entertainments (p.387).

Before we enter into any such Faustian deal, we should carefully consider the consequences. Technological events are moving rapidly. The world is already on the road to selling experiences as manufactured and metered commodities. Take sport for example. For some time sport has been in process of becoming another avenue for furthering financial interests. Television is the technical means by which the market plunders sport. Most of us who say we are 'interested' in sport don't actually play a game or even watch it as a member of a crowd. Our 'involvement' with sport is the doubly removed activity of watching it on a screen (Rodley, 1995:251). If we take sport as a metaphor for human development and social life, then more of us need to be in the game for more of the time, not paying to watch it passively from afar.

Chapter 9

THE INFORMATION SOCIETY: SELLING THE SYSTEM

Capitalism cannot live by bread alone — if 'bread' is a metaphor for the whole range of goods and services produced and sold on the market. The profit system needs the consuming time of workers as well as their producing time (Harvey, 1982:448). And to make both capitalist production and consumption possible, it needs the appropriate consenting ideas of the vast mass of the population. This consent doesn't have to take the form of active support — apathetic or even despairing acquiescence will do.

The task facing the active proponents of capitalism is to sell the system to the mass of people — most obviously at election times but implicitly at all other times. Increasingly sophisticated methods to do this are used in an increasingly 'information' society. We must first be educated (trained would be a more accurate word to describe what really goes on) to take our place in capitalist society. We must consume as much as is profitable for 'business' to sell us. The mass media of communication are there to tell us what we should think and do. The mass media and hegemonic co-operation of the subordinate mass combine to produce a culture of consumption.

So this chapter will examine four related processes designed to preserve and put an acceptable face on capitalism: education, the mass media, hegemony, and a culture of consumption.

Education

Education of the young is the first way in which they are given a foretaste of what life will be like when they reach adulthood. Most children are given a deceptively benign introduction to capitalist schooling. At first no pressure is put on them to do other than play and have their natural inquisitiveness and sense of adventure stimulated and satisfied. But this soon gives way to the real business of education. Schooling takes the place of kindergarten. Some children don't even have the benefit of kindergarten — they are thrown straight into school. Starting with first year children, a concept called 'career education' has been used to permeate all academic subjects at all levels of education:

> The whole curriculum, from start to finish, is conducted within an atmosphere of competition and stress, together with a weeding-out process which segregates those with supposedly superior talents from those less fortunate. This is accomplished through the use of tests, examinations and grading, all of which have a direct bearing upon ultimate occupations and potential earnings. Such an environment prevents the pleasurable pursuit of education as a primary end in itself. The young find themselves involved in an intensive training programme, presented under the guise of education, which will ultimately affect the price of their labour-power and in many instances can prove disastrous healthwise (Ghebre, 1994:107).

Thus schools — or at least the general run of state schools and even many of the fee-paying schools — produce minimally skilled workers for wage or salary labour. These institutions 'educate' workers to an ideology of compliance. Schools play an essential role in maintaining the status quo. 'A capitalist society requires certain general human traits and institutional features, and schools function to fulfil these demands' (Liston, 1988:16).

Education for life has long been a goal set up and discussed by teachers and others. Capitalism is increasingly eroding that role, transforming it into education for employment (or unemployment). The idea is 'that school should equip children from all social backgrounds with a greater understanding and experience of the world of work, and in the process equip them with social and technical skills required by employers' (Cohen, 1990:51).

The raw material of education — the acquisition and evaluation of knowledge — is strongly influenced by its capitalist environment. As Cohen ruefully admits, 'Really useful knowledge has come to mean skills which help you get on and make it, not insights that help you combine with others to build a better world' (1990:52). There are many ways of making money from education, but the most widespread is the use of the school as an advertising medium (Monbiot, 2000).

The privatisation of the public realm, the permeation of market values into the most intimate reaches of personal and social life, is apparent at all levels of education.

Privatisation is particularly evident in academia itself. Academics are increasingly obliged to act (and some no doubt willingly act) as agents of capital within the public sector (Slaughter and Leslie, 1997:9). They look for commercial funding for projects that are tied to national policy institutions and are partnered by prestigious firms, usually national or multinational in scope. Their own advancement is no longer dependent primarily on publications. Instead it depends at least partly on success in marketing activity. The scope of subject relevance is limited tacitly to exclude challenge of the status quo.

The University of the Third Age (U3A) is a network of voluntary educational groups catering for the 'serious leisure' needs of older people. It is proud of its emphasis on learning for its own sake, on not issuing paper qualifications linked to the labour market. I attended a U3A economics group meeting on multinational corporations and listened patiently while details of the structure and operation of those corporations were given but not examined in any critical way. I put a question which suggested that a system based on meeting need, not seeking profit, would abolish multinational corporations. I was ruled out of order. Most of the audience indicated their approval of that ruling and the rest looked sheepish. Capitalism had done a good job on them.

The mass media of communication

Before the invention of newspapers, radio and television, people had to rely for information, knowledge and entertainment mostly on unmediated interaction with other human beings. We know little about the formation of public opinion in pre-mass media times. There were teachers and preachers and grapevines along which news and views could travel. Those lines of communication still exist today, but they are overshadowed by the power of the mechanical and electronic media to tell us what is going on in the world, what politicians decide when faced with problems, and which camp the multitude should follow.

During the last few decades, and in parts of the world often described as economically developed, far-reaching social and economic changes have taken place. From having a majority of the working class making goods, the emphasis has shifted to providing services and handling information in various ways. In a word, industrial capitalism has changed to information capitalism. This doesn't mean that the exploitation of labour by capital has ceased, or even been diminished. Rather, the nature of that exploitation has changed, as Morris-Susuki (1997:65) spells out:

> Industrial capitalism, based on direct exploitation of the manufacturing workforce, is transmuted by the process of automation into a new system

where exploitation increasingly encompasses all those involved in the creation of social knowledge and in its transmission from generation to generation. Against the idea of a 'post-industrial' or 'information' society which has spontaneously and painlessly become 'post-capitalist', we can counterpose the idea of 'information capitalism' where high levels of automation and the 'softening of the economy' coexist with new and widening spheres of exploitation of the many by the few.

Ruling class ownership and control of physical capital — land, factories, railways, *etc.* — has not ended. Instead the powers and privileges associated with that ownership have been vastly increased and secured by extension of that ownership to 'information' capital (newspaper, radio and television companies, and so on). Some information is regarded by economists as a 'free good', but the means of mass communication are today certainly not free. Furthermore, those means of communication are jealously guarded by national governments on behalf of their respective ruling classes. In times of war, the television stations of the enemy are included in the targets to be 'taken out' as part of the campaign. As Coleman (1997:162) points out, the control of free speech has become more humane, but new technology has enabled it to become more subtle and effective:

> Where once power elites severed the tongues of dissenters, perhaps now the policy is to switch off the microphone; a more civilised, but no less undemocratic, form of gagging. If the modern resistance to unregulated discussion, in Britain if not elsewhere, draws the line well short of massacring workers in Manchester or surrounding the Hyde Park gates with police, we have yet to see what response there would be for a struggle for equal access to and control of the contemporary means of mass communication.

The interests of information capital seem to be best served, not by denying workers all access to the media, but by allowing selected small minorities of them to have a piece of the action, to give the semblance of some measure of free speech. Thus we have phone-in radio programmes which purport to be 'the voice of the nation'. But, as Coleman (1997:125) notes, 'Phone-ins often accentuate the gulf between the authoritative expert and the humbly questioning laity.' Television consumer watchdog programmes serve the same deceptive purpose. A few customers have their complaints against inefficient or unscrupulous companies upheld and compensated for. This is designed to strengthen our confidence in making purchases where we are subject only to normal, rather than exceptional, exploitation.

Defenders of the mass media point to the choice available to consumers as justification for its increasing role in telling us what to think and what to buy. But the 500 television channels promised for every household will bring only an illusion of variety and choice (Martin and Schumann, 1997;18). Choice at the margin hides denial of choice at the core. If all candidates at an election stand only for slightly different ways of running capitalism, then those who wish to reject the profit system and live in some other kind of society are given no choice at all.

A mass in its most human form is happily co-operative, giving and taking, sharing, creative in its actions and experiences, stressing the indissoluble nature of the individual and society. A mass in its least human form is cruelly competitive, isolated, ignorant, easily inflamed by base emotions, elevating and glorifying the individual above society, empowering and blindly following power-hungry and often psychopathic leaders to destructive ends.

Profit society likes things to be privatised, not socialised. Business-friendly governments — there is no other kind — promote the mass communication industry. According to Keane (1991:192), privatisation of the means of communication under state control:

> is likely to penetrate the heart of everyday life — reshaping our language, our sense of time and space, our basic likes and loves. It may be that citizens will no longer invest any hopes in public life. Perhaps they will amuse themselves to death, spending their spare time 'grazing' the new abundance of pre-censored, commercialized radio, television, newspapers and magazines. Perhaps they will be persuaded to privatize themselves, to regard politics as a nuisance, to transform themselves silently and unprotestingly from citizens to mobile and private consumers.

One of the most popular types of radio and television programme is the soap opera. The label 'soap opera' was first attached to dramatic sagas broadcast by American radio in the 1930s. Drama of this sort was found to be the cheapest way of filling in the gaps between the commercials for detergents which sponsored the shows. The business has expanded enormously. Every week the studios receive messages of love, hate, advice and enquiry about people who do not exist. Soap operas are worthy of close critical analysis, and Jay (1986:167) offers just that:

> Most soap operas, for most of the time, play a part in confirming social prejudices which support capitalism. Implicit in the drama, or as the critics

say 'written into the sub-text', are all sorts of notions about the world we live in... They include the ideas that people suffer from something horrible called 'human nature' — an incurable condition that can only be softened or controlled but never removed. It means that people are innately anti-social or irrational. Other assumptions include the idea that the majority of people are not intelligent or responsible enough to exist socially without bosses, political leaders and police forces to keep them in order.

The role of soap operas in promoting acquiescence in the profit system is also recognised by Chomsky (1998:370), who links that role with the electoral process and the public education system, both of which have the same goal:

> The citizens in a capitalist democracy must be diverted by emotionally potent oversimplifications, marginalized, and isolated. Ideally, each person should be alone in front of the television screen, watch sports, soap operas or commercials, deprived of organizational structures that permit individuals lacking resources to discover what they think and believe in interaction with others, to formulate their own concerns and programs, and to act to realise them. They can be permitted, even encouraged, to ratify the decisions of their betters in periodic elections. The rascal multitude are the proper targets of the mass media and a public education system geared to obedience and training in needed skills, including the skill of repeating patriotic slogans on timely occasions.

If individuals are isolated when subject to largely one-way communication, they are cut off from sources which could challenge the validity of the overt and covert messages received. The audiences for soap operas, newspaper stories and political pronouncements are guided subtly towards conformity. They are made to feel uncomfortable about challenging anything beyond the superficial differences in what is presented to them. Stratman (n.d.:49) sums up this situation:

> The media generate a kind of false community, dominated by corporate values and corporate images of the world. To join your fellow humans in this community, all you have to do is surrender your real feelings and values to agree with whatever it is that the media say that other people think... however contemptuous of the politicians and corporate leaders who parade across the screen, however a person feels about the reality presented by the media, he can still be made to feel that 'nobody feels this way but me'.

Hegemony

Discussion of the mass media leads us to consider another and related feature of capitalist society, the way in which its victims are persuaded to cooperate in their own exploitation. It is one thing to have a substantial part of your labour power stolen from you, to endure poverty, wars, environmental degradation, and so on. It is quite another thing to be convinced that there is no alternative to things being that way, that no changes but the most superficial ones are worth the effort of even thinking about. That craftily critical supporter of capitalism, Galbraith, taunts us with the observation that 'the controlling contentment and resulting belief is now that of the many, not just of the few' (1993:10).

Marx can be forgiven for not having recognised and analysed the ways in which hegemony has come to play such an important part in the sustenance and development of capitalism. In his day the information society was in its infancy. Poorly educated workers, without the vote and subject to a more brutal form of class and property society than we have today, could more easily have felt that it was *their* system, not *ours*. A number of writers have contributed to our understanding of what hegemony is and how it works. I start with one of the clearest statements, perhaps an unlikely find in a book mainly about leisure:

> Hegemony entails class domination through the participation of subordinate classes. In our daily work and leisure activities we participate in creating the conditions and social relations that shape our lives... Hegemony varies in strength; it is never total, secure, complete but is susceptible to attack, degeneration, undermining, displacement. A practice is hegemonic to the degree that its structure is defined by elites, by centralized social structures, and even by the physical space and objects available for the practice — relative to being controlled by its practitioners. A study of the commercialisation of leisure reveals how that part of our lived experience supposed to be free of domination is transformed by capitalist development. The expropriation of the means of leisure is a prerequisite for commercialization... A generation that grows up with purchased leisure may not develop the skills of self-entertainment (Butsch, 1990:8).

Butsch goes on to describe how most contemporary leisure practices are not entirely the impositions of profit-seeking capital, nor are they entirely the free expression of what consumers want. They are a combination of both. Ideas for new products, services and experiences are not simply reflections of capitalism but are also mass-mediated expressions of people. Consumers participate in shaping new products and practices, which corporations in turn shape into profitable sales and supporting mass culture.

Some years ago Gorz (1966:328) recognised the hegemonic nature of capitalism and the vital role that workers play in keeping it going: 'Workers endorse the employers' power every day, by clocking in on time, by submitting to work which they have no hand in organising, by taking home pay-packets... Modern industry's dominant tendency is no longer the maximum exploitation of the workers. The dominant tendency is to 'integrate' the workers into the system.'

For capitalism to stagger from one crisis to the next, to alternate between boom and slump, to produce extremes of wealth and poverty, but to provide tolerable conditions for most of the people most of the time, it is not necessary that everyone wholeheartedly supports the system. It is better for 'stability' that the way things are organised and controlled is not even seen as a system, as one possibility among others. The commitment of subordinates to the system is likely to take the form mostly of pragmatic acquiescence rather than normative or ideological involvement (Hill, 1990:3). However keen on the ideology of the profit system its beneficiaries and apologists may be, however wise they may appear to be in selecting for support the best of all possible systems, it is safer for them to rely on TINA ('there is no alternative'), as Miliband (1994:11) spells out:

> Hegemony... is usually taken to mean the capacity of ruling classes to instil their values into subordinate classes and to turn these values into the 'common sense of the epoch'. By now, hegemony has acquired an additional meaning: it must also be taken to mean the capacity of ruling classes to persuade subordinate classes that, whatever they may think of the social order, and however much they may be alienated from it, there is no alternative to it. Hegemony depends not so much on consent as on resignation.

Kolakowski (1978:242) carries the argument a stage further, echoing and developing the Marxist claim that the prevailing ideas of the time are those of the ruling class, formulated and disseminated as a result of that class's ownership and control of the intellectual and cultural as well as the physical means of production. He also outlines the challenge facing workers to overcome the prevailing status-quo culture and to substitute a revolutionary and egalitarian culture:

> ... hegemony signifies the control of the intellectual life of society by purely cultural means. Every class tries to secure a governing position not only in public institutions but also in regard to the opinions, values and standards acknowledged by the bulk of society. The privileged classes in their time secured a position of hegemony in the intellectual as well as the political sphere; they subjugated the others by this means, and intellectual supremacy was a precondition of political rule. The main task of the workers in modern times was to liberate themselves spiritually from the culture of the bourgeoisie.

But the challenge has not been met and hegemony persists. The bourgeois culture extends far beyond intellectual life and politics. It permeates education, the family, everyday life, work and leisure. No aspect of social structure and individual life is untouched by capitalist values, though they may be resisted. If those values are ubiquitous today we must remember that they have not always existed and need not exist indefinitely into the future.

A culture of consumption

> Historians and archaeologists will one day discover that the ads of our time are the richest and most faithful reflections that any society ever made of its entire range of activities.
> Marshall McLuhan

> The incessant witless repetition of advertisers' moron-fodder has become so much a part of life that if we are not careful, we forget to be insulted by it.
> *The Times*

These quotes, appearing among others on the back cover of a book by Robinson (1998), illustrate from different points of view the pervasive role that the process of persuading us to consume performs in capitalist society. Advertising is part of this process, but so are the associated 'industries' of marketing, market research, public relations, lobbying, think tanks, image and presentation consultancies, consumer advice and protection bodies and programmes (Beder, 2000:276). Late capitalism is increasingly a culture of consumption. Shop till you drop is a popular injunction (perhaps buy till you die is too morbid an idea to be successfully marketed).

There is profit in selling things to people who cannot really afford to buy them but can be enticed, cajoled or shamed into buying them. There is even more profit in concentrating sales efforts on people with money who can be more easily lured into buying things they don't need but can be persuaded to want. Battery-powered dancing beer cans and waterproof bible cases are available to American consumers. In Japan you can buy a doll which precisely resembles your own child (you're never too young to become a customer).

The culture of consumption is one example of hegemony. It creates realms of negotiation and empowerment in the consumption and interpretations that sustain the legitimacy of domination. Even trends of protest in fashion, film, music, travel and leisure soon become mass-marketed for privatized consumption (Mosbacher, 2002).

The importance to capitalism of our role as consumers is evident in the huge amount of time, effort and money that goes into monitoring our buying habits, 'lifestyle' choices and financial stature (Staples, 1997:81). Apparently one consulting firm sneaks tiny cameras inside frozen-food compartments in supermarkets to chart the eye movements of shoppers in the hope of determining better placement for high-margin items (Robinson, 1998:114).

We are cast as accomplices in our own commercial seduction. Every time we hand out information about ourselves we are feeding databases with more details. Every time we buy something with a credit card we leave a breadcrumb on the trail of our consumer habits. Such crumbs of information are diligently saved, analysed, processed and disseminated by market research sparrows. Their conclusions affect the mail offers we receive, the telemarketing calls we get, what products go on our local supermarket shelves.

The culture of consumption depends very largely on the use of technology for its maintenance and development. In theory, technology is neutral regarding the type of society we live in. We should be as able to use technology for revolutionary purposes as for status quo purposes. But the vital decisions about technology are not in neutral hands. They are in the hands of those who benefit most from the present arrangements.

Early in the twentieth century the technology of Taylorism was used to make factory production more profitable. Work operations were broken down, speeded up, priced more economically to the employer. Mattelart (1979:175) suggests that the norms of Taylorism have invaded the educational sphere: they preside over the tightening up of the ideological apparatus to watch over the commercial potential of young minds.

An adequate understanding of capitalism, undertaking not merely to understand it but more importantly to surpass it, requires understanding the various social forces that hold it together, the complex intermingling and reciprocity of politics, prevailing ideology, property rights, the functions of money, mass media, education, and much else. Bocock (1986:33) makes an admirable attempt to survey this vast field, in a passage which I locate here rather than elsewhere in the book because he concludes with the formation of the desire to consume goods and services, in other words the culture of consumption:

> The workers, and others, hold the values and political ideas that they do as a consequence of both trying to survive, and of attempting to enjoy themselves, within capitalism. These activities require money; the cash nexus remains, therefore, a major means of social, economic and political control. The control exerted by the cash nexus is mediated by ideological means, for people have to come to desire the goods offered for sale. Such desires are not natural or inborn, and they are not taken for granted by modern capitalism. The desires to consume various products have to be constructed by ideological apparatuses, especially in the mass media — not only by explicit advertisements but more especially through the portrayal of life-styles in stories, films, articles, photographs and television images. No revolution led by the proletariat of the Western capitalist societies is in sight on this view, as long as their desires to consume goods and services are being formed in this way.

It would be dangerously close to a single issue approach to a complex world to believe that workers' consuming desires and habits are the only, or even the main, thing standing in the way of their joining a revolution to abolish capitalism and replace it with a system more worthy of their potential development. However, there is much evidence that capitalism does lead us to depend on consuming for our happiness and our sense of self ('I consume, therefore I am').

There is nothing wrong with seeking to satisfy your own authentic needs, the needs of others and of the community and society in which you live. But there is something seriously wrong with a society that is based so firmly on commercial relationships and fosters a culture of consumption in which the basic needs of much of the world's population remain unmet. Even under the pressures of capitalism, we are not just buyers and sellers, exploited and exploiters. Acts of giving and taking, sharing, co-operating, going out of one's way to help others, are not usually prominent when 'human nature' is discussed. But such acts are there to be maximised in a new society where consumerism will be a thing of the past.

Chapter 10

ENVIRONMENTAL DEGRADATION

More irreversible damage has been done to the natural environment by human action during the last hundred years than in any previous period in recorded history. The list of problems is long and growing, including global warming, greenhouse gas emissions, air and water pollution, depletion of the ozone layer, acid rain, deforestation, desertification, loss of biodiversity, overfishing, the hunting of certain animals to extinction, and disposal of nuclear waste. Most of these problems are caused or made worse by the dominance of short-term profit seeking over long-term sustainability.

I first try to summarise the various elements of the problem. To do so adequately would fill a book much larger than this one, so I offer only a broad-brush picture. The second section deals with the ecological or green movement and the solutions its members propose to the various problems without linking such solutions to a policy of replacing capitalism with socialism (though some of the people I quote may feel that they are implicitly red as well as green). Lastly I look at the writers who are explicitly red and green, who recognise that environmental problems will not be effectively tackled as a single issue but must be seen as part of a whole world system that needs to be replaced.

Extent of the problem

Some environmental problems will arise on Earth whatever the social, economic and political system. Earthquakes and volcanoes are examples, although even in these cases the effects can be mitigated by human intervention or worsened by failure to intervene. At present, economic pressures force some people to live closer to danger areas than if the avoidance of death and injury had a higher priority than property considerations. Drought and floods are to some extent natural occurrences but their effects on humans and the environment have been made worse by methods of production, extraction and cultivation that have put more emphasis on short-term gain than on long-term sustainability.

Much of the literature on the extent of environmental degradation deals with it as a problem arising from the relentless pursuit of material growth. The market system encourages mass consumption which in turn leads to damage to the natural environment. Greider (1997:52) poses the rhetorical question 'In crude terms, if everyone owns a car and refrigerator, if every nation becomes rich enough to throw off vast quantities of industrial waste, can the earth stand it?' To argue in this way is not to deny that modern industry has produced goods that have added to the material comfort and convenience of some of the people. Nor is it to oppose the efforts of those in the economically underdeveloped or developing countries to share in such a materially enriched life. But it is to point out that, if unchecked, the environmental consequences of unremitting 'growth' will one day overwhelm everyone, rich and poor alike.

A more sensible policy would be to pursue a sustainable society, along the lines advocated by Meadows and his colleagues (1992:210): 'A sustainable society would be interested in qualitative development, not physical expansion. It would use material growth as a considered tool, not as a perpetual mandate... A sustainable society would apply its values and its best knowledge of the earth's limits to choose only those kinds of growth that would actually serve social goals and enhance sustainability.'

With developments in technology, the number of ways in which humans are adversely affecting the environment is proliferating (Goudie, 2000:420). The complexity, frequency and magnitude of impacts on the environment is increasing, partly because of the growth in population and partly because those more people are consuming more things. Experts disagree about the rate of harmful change, but no one doubts that the changes are taking place. Lomborg (2001) calls himself a sceptical environmentalist because some past predictions (for example, the number of species becoming extinct) were shown to have been exaggerated. But he doesn't deny that global warming is taking place, making only a lower estimate of the future increase in global temperature than other experts.

The capitalist accounting system makes no provision to pay for the preservation of the planet. The short time-scale of giant corporations, under constant pressure to produce profits for shareholders, is inevitably at odds with the long-term needs of conservation and environmental protection (Sampson, 1989:201). Again, people in the poorest countries suffer most from this process. The richer countries are able to export pollution by moving production to Third World countries where environmental standards are looser. The 'advanced' countries remain relatively clean at the cost of other parts of the world becoming dirtier (Gray, 1998:81).

Capitalism teaches us to exploit the Earth and its environment as well as each other. The tools for this purpose are various technologies, and the aim is profit for the few. Worster (1988:11) sums up what has happened:

> The capitalists and their theoreticians promised that through the technological domination of the earth they could deliver a more fair, rational, efficient, and productive life for everyone, themselves above all. Their method was simply to free individual enterprise from the bonds of traditional hierarchy and community, whether the bonding derived from other humans or the environment. That meant teaching everyone to treat the earth, as well as each other, with a frank, energetic self-assertiveness, unembarrassed by too many moral or aesthetic sentiments. To behave otherwise must be tantamount to failure as a human being. People must begin to work and produce not for the purpose of meeting their own family and community needs directly, but for selling to others, more often than not to strangers, and must then buy whatever was needed... They must think constantly in terms of making money. They must regard everything around them — the land, its natural resources, their own labour — as potential commodities that might fetch a profit in the market.

The individual pursuit of wealth, considered as the driving force of society, leads to degradation of the natural environment as inevitably as it leads to the exploitation of people (Taylor, 1992:186). This situation is exemplified by what has come to be called the tragedy of the commons. It is in everybody's interests to stop the fouling of air, earth and water. But so long as this is only a matter of individual decision, it is in no individual's clear and obvious interest to do so, if others are unlikely to follow suit.

Green but not red

In the face of extensive and increasing environmental degradation, an influential ecological or 'green' movement has responded with a number of proposals to mitigate, if not solve, the problem. I shall deal in the next section with the 'green' proposals which are linked with 'red' proposals to change the overall system. But first we should look at the greens who either say nothing about systemic change or actually make it clear that they don't advocate or support such change.

Porritt (1984), a British establishment figure with Royal Family connections, is a good green to start with. Like many others who think along similar lines, for him the enemy is the mismanagement of industrialism, not the capitalist system. Green politics is 'neither right nor left, nor in the centre' (p.43). Porritt claims to reject the ideologies of both capitalism and communism, but he means by the latter the system that prevailed in the Soviet Union at the time he was writing. What he calls the super-ideology of industrialism he believes 'is itself the greatest threat we face' (p.44). It is clear that Porritt doesn't reject capitalism, although he is a keen reformer of it. Among 14 of his minimum criteria for being green is 'lasting security to be achieved through non-nuclear defence strategies and considerably reduced arms spending' (p.10). A proposal to delight non-red greens, Fabians, *etc.* — but certainly not socialists.

It is clear from his several books that Bookchin is an opponent of capitalism, but he makes a point of asserting that 'the color of radicalism today is no longer red; it is green...' (1986:45). Bookchin is a strange mixture of the revolutionary and the reformist, but (as we shall see more fully in chapter 14) in any combination of the two the reformist becomes dominant and the revolutionary recessive. Bookchin writes eloquently of the substitution of economy for society, the ascendancy of the buyer-seller relationship, and the networks of mutual aid and reciprocity that capitalism has destroyed. But he puts his faith in grassroots politics, 'fertilized by the ecological, feminist, communitarian, and antiwar movements that have patently displaced the traditional workers' movements of half a century ago' (p.45). While it is true that the workers' movements to which he refers contained very few revolutionaries, the same has to be said of contemporary ecological, feminist, communitarian and antiwar movements.

You don't have to be explicitly pro-green and anti-red in order to be effectively only green. You just have to concentrate on environmental problems, their extent and possible solution or at least alleviation, and say nothing about the wider social, economic and political system in which they are embedded. Many, but by no means all, greens do this. Large corporations are quite willing to debate environmental issues with campaigners so long as final decisions about what they produce and how they produce it remain under their control. Korten (1995:307) makes no bones about pointing out that 'the guiding principles of the Ecological Revolution are actively pro-business and pro-market, but they favour local over global businesses and markets.'

Red and green

The greatest red of all time (or at least thinker of the second millennium), Karl Marx, is sometimes accused of lacking greenness. Certainly he devoted less attention to environmental problems than most socialists do today. But that is partly because the extent and severity of those problems was less in his time than in ours. However, he and Engels were well aware of the damaging consequences of capitalist control of the industrial system, both to people and to their environment. This is made clear in a recent study by Burkett (1999), *Marx and Nature: A Red and Green Perspective*. The following statement by Engels (1940:290) is evidence that he was an early eco-socialist:

> Let us not, however, flatter ourselves overmuch on account of our human conquest of nature. For each such conquest takes its revenge on us... Thus at every step we are reminded that we by no means rule over nature like a conqueror over a foreign people, like someone standing outside nature — but that we, with flesh, blood and brain, belong to nature, and exist in its midst, and that all our mastery over nature consists in the fact that we have the advantage over all other beings of being able to know and correctly apply its laws.

Eco-socialists argue that capitalism has an inbuilt preference for ecologically damaging technologies because they provide increases in the productivity of saleable goods per unit of labour (Burgmann, 1993:236). For the same reason, ecologically benign technologies and pollution controls will be rejected by capitalism because they do not add to the value of saleable goods. Burgmann is also critical of what she calls 'people power' which consists not of mass collective protest aimed at changing the system, but rather in atomised individuals encouraging companies to carry on business as usual but to make their profits in less dangerous ways (p.240).

In contrast to the views of Korten quoted above, Cotgrove (1982) believes that the radical environmentalist movement from the late 1960s has provided a vehicle for the resurgence of an anti-business culture (p.111). But he does recognise the revolutionary limitations of an environmental movement that is concerned only with the environment: 'Although their beliefs point to the need for social transformation, environmentalists have generally failed to go on to make the necessary analysis of the structural changes which would be necessary' (p.113). In his discussion of politics, Cotgrove emerges as a social democrat rather than a socialist. However, for him the general thrust of environmentalism is utopian, and utopian thought presents the possibility of an alternative future.

Pepper (1993) considers the combination of red and green critically and at some length. Starting with a concern for environmental issues, he is convinced that greens need to assimilate Marxist perspectives into their analysis. He is critical of greens who are not red; their political approach is 'pragmatic and eclectic'. He supports the views of the Socialist Party of Great Britain on environmental issues (1990) and quotes those views (expressed in publications and tapes) extensively. However, Pepper's commitment to socialism is weakened by his description of the SPGB as 'Marxist purists' and by his apparent acceptance of Tony Benn's insubstantial definition of the basic principles of socialism as 'equity, democracy, accountability, internationalism and morality' (p.2). If that is all socialism means then capitalism will have little difficulty in remaining in business.

Part II — SOCIALISM

Chapter 11

A BRIEF HISTORY OF SOCIALIST IDEAS

In order to survey the history of socialist ideas we must first have some criteria for deciding what to count as contributions to socialist ideas. I don't think it's sensible to aim at inclusivity, certainly not in the sense of giving equal weight to different interpretations. Therefore I propose to concentrate on those contributions to socialist theory and possible future practice which clearly demarcate socialism from all forms of property and class society, most notably capitalism.

I start with historical campaigns and movements. Although socialism as a word was born only in the early 19th century, it seems reasonable to trace its ancestry much farther back than that. So I trace what might be called pre-visions of socialism back to the earliest struggles for equality and co-operation in class-divided societies. During the last two centuries, socialism has moved from being unthought of to being subject to a wide variety of interpretations.

The literary contributions to socialist ideas take a number of different forms. Some tales are more or less autobiographical — Tressell's *The Ragged Trousered Philanthropists*, for example. The socialism in these tales is implicit, embedded in personal experience of the problems and sometimes the horrors of capitalism. More provocative are the scenarios — predictions of what socialism will be like as a world to live in and a community to be fashioned and shared and enjoyed. In my view Morris's *News from Nowhere* remains the classic example of this genre.

Contemporary contributions to socialist ideas come from different sources, some academic, some more practical. Psychologists and anthropologists offer evidence that a misconceived 'human nature' is no barrier to socialism. There are proto-socialist practices to be seen within capitalism — blood donation, for instance. Subsistence for everyone and voluntary simplicity are relevant ideas and practices.

Finally we have a mixed bag of authors who seek to foist on to socialism ideas and ways of behaving which are really versions — usually quite nasty versions — of capitalism. They may purport to be friends of socialism, but are in fact its enemies.

Historical campaigns and movements

It makes no more sense to speculate about who was the first socialist than about who first introduced slavery or feudalism or capitalism to the world. Although no socialist system has existed at any time or place on earth (socialism is essentially a world society) we speak today quite reasonably of socialists, people who hold and propagate ideas relevant to a system yet to come. We do so because humans, unlike all other animals, are able to raise in their imagination a structure which they have yet to bring into being.

Most historians agree that the term socialism was coined, initially in France and Britain, in the 1830s. But ideas don't suddenly leap out of history fully formed. They grow from earlier ideas and are shaped by the society in which they develop. Paczuska (1986:6) suggests that the vision of equality and co-operation which was called socialism in the early 1800s has been with us, in one form or another, for a very much longer time. As long as we are clear that such pre-visions of socialism are no more than that — the idea in its infancy rather than its maturity — then we may try to trace its evolution.

Two main themes are evident in the ancient history of the socialist idea — revolt against oppression and utopia as the ideal society. There were many slave rebellions in the ancient world, of which the most famous were led by Spartacus from 73 BC on. Slave armies initially defeated the Roman regular troops, but eventually they were themselves defeated. This did not stop slave revolts elsewhere. Paczuska (p.10) quotes an Arab writer describing one African uprising:

> They hate the master and the rich, and when they meet a master riding in his chariot and surrounded by his slaves, they make him get down, put the slaves in the chariot, and oblige their masters to run on foot. They boast that they have come to re-establish equality on earth, and they summon the slaves to liberty.

With the coming of feudalism the peasantry followed the tradition set by the slaves. In the early 14th century the Black Death caused an acute labour shortage. Peasants saw their chance to demand better wages, an end to manorial dues, and the right to change jobs. In 1381 they took direct action, urged on by radical preachers such as John Ball, who rallied them with a call to end the class system:

> Good people, things cannot go right in England and never will, until goods are held in common and there are no more villeins and gentlefolk, but we are all one and the same (Froissart, 1968:212).

The Peasants' Revolt was savagely crushed and the exploitation of landless peasants continued, as did periodic revolts. Movements like those of the Levellers and the Diggers came to the fore during the so-called English Revolution of the 1640s. In Winstanley's words, 'The poorest man has as true a title, as just a right, to land as a rich man' (Paczuska, p.16).

Mixed up with the struggle against exploitation was the dream of a better world, or utopia. In Britain in the middle ages the dream land was called Cockaygne, but elsewhere it had other names and variations on a common theme. It was a happy place, with no hierarchy, no work and no worry. But sometimes the dreamers seemed to have one foot in the world of property relationships ('Every man may drink his fill/And needn't sweat to pay the bill').

Thomas More's *Utopia*, published in Latin in 1516, is arguably an early contribution to socialist thought. On More's imaginary island private property has been abolished and everybody takes equal turns to work on the land. But prisoners of war, convicted criminals and religious zealots do the dirty work so their 'betters' can be equal (rather like the slaves in Plato's Republic). Like most utopians, More seems not to have understood that people can only win freedom for themselves.

The French Revolution of 1789 held out great expectations for advocates of an equal society at that time. It was a mass popular movement against the decaying feudal order. United round the slogan 'Liberty, equality and fraternity', Parisians overthrew the king and France became a republic. But the leadership of the movement was seized by the Jacobins, who represented the interests of the rising merchant (bourgeois) class. The profit system survived, was superficially changed, but the hopes of the few contemporary socialists were dashed.

The call to revolution was echoed in the French colonies (notably in the

Caribbean) but with the same result: exploitation of the masses by means of slavery and serfdom gave way to wage slavery. English radical republicanism found expression in Tom Paine's *The Rights of Man*, published in 1791. Paine argued that people should be free to choose their own government, but his proposals, which included cutting spending on armed forces and bureaucracy, were essentially reformist rather than revolutionary.

The developing Industrial Revolution produced a reaction among workers who saw the new machines as depriving them of independent work and forcing them to accept starvation wages and massive unemployment. The Luddites resorted to smashing machines rather than smashing the system that exploited them. While some skilled workers supported the Luddites, others put their faith in the ancient craft unions or guilds which had existed from the middle ages. This led to the formation of the guild socialism movement, also known as associative democracy. Hirst (1994:103) explains that, according to this doctrine, 'the nation would be the ultimate owner of all major productive property and land. However, the national guilds would hold that property in trust, and have effective possession of it while they provided a service to society and the consumer.' The resemblance of this to the later Labour Party's nationalisation policies is obvious.

The early 19th century saw a resurgence of the utopian movement, particularly in Britain and France. Robert Owen, a wealthy industrialist, set up a model factory at New Lanark in Scotland. He limited the hours of work, provided decent housing and education, and established a co-operative store. He is reputed to have coined the word 'socialism' to describe his experiment. But all he communities founded by Owen and his followers failed. Capitalism was not to be overthrown by good intentions and philanthropy.

Utopian proposals in France were similarly tainted with the status quo. Saint-Simon was against war, organised religion, racial intolerance and social oppression. But his plans were for a rigidly organised and highly centralised society run by experts. Fourier's 'socialism' was similarly flawed. He favoured communes ('phalansteries') in which people would be free to do the work they wanted. He believed in equal rights for women and had enlightened views on education. But the communities that were set up to put his ideas into practice (chiefly in America) failed to last very long. The same has to be said about later communes based on various ideological beliefs (Bang, 1987:101).

Two other movements in the first half of the 19th century deserve mention: Chartism and the trade unions. Chartism has been called the first independent movement of the working class, but its aims were extremely limited: universal manhood suffrage and a number of related electoral reforms. The idea survives today in such organisations as Charter 88, a force for greater democracy while at no point challenging the basic capitalist system. Trade unions represented, and still represent, the collective interest of organised workers within the profit system, but again in no way do they pose a threat to that system.

The arrival of Marx and Engels on the political scene was a giant step forward for socialist ideas, primarily as an outstanding critique of capitalism and secondarily as a call for its replacement by socialism/communism. Below I devote a whole chapter to Marxian ideas on socialism. Following Marx and Engels there were a number of campaigns and movements associated with the concept of socialism. The Paris Commune of 1871 was a remarkable example of workers' ability to organise democratically in their own interest. It lasted two months but was defeated by a combination of repressive force and internal lack of sufficient socialist consciousness.

In the second half of the 19th century various reformers, radicals and self-styled socialists increased their numbers and influence. In 1881 the Democratic Federation was founded, followed in 1884 by the Social Democratic Federation. The uneasy coalition between those supporting a 'minimum programme' (reforms of capitalism) and a 'maximum programme' (socialist revolution) was broken in 1904 by the formation of the Socialist Party of Great Britain (Perrin, 2000:12).

The rest is modern history... Companion Parties of the SPGB have been formed in a number of countries around the world, and the SPGB will soon have reached its centenary. Apart from this nascent and admittedly small World Socialist Movement, the 20th century 'contributions' to socialism have been at best confusing and at worst cruelly deceptive. The Soviet revolution promised first socialism and then communism but delivered only state capitalism. Social democracy's way of administering capitalism has proved more durable. Old Labour used 'socialism' for a future to be kept at a safe distance. New Labour's hegemony (see chapter 9) decided that it has more to lose than gain by paying even lip service to the s-word.

Literary contributions

Literary contributions to socialism are of two main kinds — autobiographical or anecdotal (mostly critical of capitalism) and predictive of socialism.

Among works of the first type Tressell's *The Ragged Trousered Philanthropists* (1956) and Jack London's *The Iron Heel* (n.d.) are two of the best known. Tressell was a housepainter who wrote about the lives and opinions of a group of working men in the building trade. He saw his book as a novel, not a treatise. His descriptions of people, places and situations are very good; his characters discuss socialism, but only vaguely as an aspiration. London's tale is of class struggle in early 20th century New York. His book title derives from the capitalist's threat 'We will grind you revolutionists down under our heel, and we shall walk upon your faces' (p.75).

Zinn's short play, *Marx in Soho* (1999) is a splendid, fact-based speculative bit of biography. Marx finds himself by mistake in Soho, New York instead of London, attempting to refute the rumour that his ideas are dead. The labour theory of value, the materialist conception of history, and the class struggle are all discussed in fairly simple terms. And Marx's projected views on Stalin are forthright: 'Do they think that a system run by a thug who murdered his fellow revolutionaries is communism?'

Then the more future-oriented contributions. Oscar Wilde produced only one essay on socialism (*The Soul of Man Under Socialism*, 1912) but it is deservedly rated very highly. Edgar (2000) discusses it, noting a number of quotes of which this is typical: 'why should [the poor] be grateful for the crumbs that fall from the rich man's table? They should be seated at the board, and are beginning to know it.'

Ursula Le Guin's *The Dispossessed* (1974) may be seen as a social science fiction contribution to socialism. Her two worlds Urras and Anarras refer to the USA and an idealised Soviet Union. At a number of points she describes the socialism of Anarras: 'Nothing is yours. It is to use. It is to share' (p.22); '... there's no government on Anarras. However, obviously there's administration' (p.61).

In *The Last Capitalist* (1996) the author, Steve Cullen, has Anne Riordan, writing in the first person, on the trail of a mysterious man reputed to be trying to restore capitalism in a future anarchist world. 'Atopia' is in some ways like Morris's socialist future. People work at what they like doing and what is useful to the community. No one has weapons except as museum pieces. They have free access to beer and public transport, but still think in terms of exchange and barter. No capitalist money, but they do have a Work Scrip system. Cullen's Atopia is a pleasant enough world, but its people seem unwilling to give up capitalist calculation.

From different sources

Ideas about socialism come from many different sources. Some may be called 'academic', suggesting that they derive from an intellectual development and exchange of thought. Others stem from lived experience, the ways in which people do treat each other in 'socialist' ways, even within capitalism. There is no rigid dividing line between the two types of source. Thought leads to corresponding action, and the results of action provoke further thought. So we have many and varied contributions, some lengthy and significant, some brief and perhaps hardly worth a mention. The following sources are admittedly selective, though hopefully fairly representative.

The ideas of some anarchists have much in common with those of socialists. Without going into detail in support of that proposition, I cite one anarchist, Kropotkin (1972) who wrote at length about mutual aid in village life, labour unions, strikes and slum life. He showed that mutual aid is a deeply human form of co-operation, repressed though it often is in capitalism. It will surely come into its own in socialism.

Kohn (1990), an American psychologist, endorses and gives further examples of Kropotkin's approach. Even within capitalism, we help strangers just because they need helping, not because we expect to gain anything out of it. Kohn's views on human nature are essentially socialist: 'We invoke it to explain selfishness rather than service, competition rather than cooperation, egocentricity rather than empathy' (p.3). He looks to a socialist future, but in a typically understated way: '... social structures predicated on human selfishness have no claim to inevitability' (p.4).

In commenting on the ideas about consumption held by early socialist thinkers, Thompson (2001:68) observes that 'For them consumption was to be above all else an expression of social purpose and a celebration of society's achievements, not a degrading, desperate and self-regarding assertion of personal identity.'

The theme of willingness to help others without reward is taken up by Titmus (1971). He quotes a survey in which over 80 percent of people donating blood said they did so for various reasons unconnected with personal gain. This led Titmus to conclude that 'the ways in which society organizes and structures its social institutions — and particularly its health and welfare systems — can encourage or discourage the altruism in man; such systems can foster integration or alienation...' (p.225). There is no doubt which system Titmus prefers. On the same theme, McCaughey (1997:162) reminds us that

'The gift relationship, the implementation of social policy that cannot be left to market forces or thought of only in economic terms, covers large areas of our lives, touches many people, in some ways touches us all... The gift relationship is not complete until all parties see themselves as recipients and as contributors. Everyone has a need, and everyone has something to offer. A civilized society will recognize both.'

A further source of socialist ideas is the question of what will replace capitalist values and world views. The apparent polar opposite of the consuming life is the life of poverty. But there is another way of looking at the opposite of consumerism. That way is what Elgin and Mitchell (1977) call 'voluntary simplicity', living in a way that is outwardly simple and inwardly rich. When contrasted with the capitalist world view, some features of voluntary simplicity are:

- people with nature instead of people over nature
- smaller, less complex living and working environments instead of large, complex ones
- identity found through inner and interpersonal discovery instead of defined by patterns of consumption
- laid back, relaxed life instead of high pressure, rat race existence

Socialism does not mean that everyone will live as the rich do today — that would neither be possible nor desirable. In the words of Mies and Bennholdt-Thomsen (1999:4), 'The utopia of a socialist society cannot be modelled on the lifestyle of the ruling classes... rather it must be based on subsistence security for everybody.'

'With friends like that...'

A simple inventory of writings on socialism would include 'contributions' not only from people who see it as a mere variant of capitalism but also who are deeply opposed to socialism as a revolutionary, non-capitalist world system. The confusion caused by those who aim to destroy or at least damage the socialist movement by misrepresentation explains the full title of this section; 'With friends like that, who needs enemies?'

The numbers of socialism's false friends are quite large and their views well publicised. Their pronouncements are often similar to each other, so the following are examples rather than a full list.

A great variety of ideas, proposals and schemes have been associated with the label 'socialism'. In 1956 Crosland assembled and briefly discussed 12 'socialist doctrines': the philosophy of natural law, Owenism, the labour theory of value, Christian socialism, Marxism, the theory of rent as unearned increment, Morris and anti-commercialism, Fabianism, the ILP tradition, the Welfare State or paternalist tradition, syndicalism and guild socialism, and the doctrine of planning (pp.81–7).

Crosland presents this tremendous range of different ideas even-handedly, as if he were simply discussing flavours of ice-cream. Many of his doctrines are, of course, contained comfortably within capitalism. He does an injustice to Morris's socialism when he restricts it to anti-commercialism. Marxism, not qualified, is at least not distorted. But by diluting and muddling the meaning of socialism so comprehensively, Crosland reveals himself as no friend of it.

Many of the definitions of socialism put forward by those who are clearly not its friends describe programmes advocated by Old Labour (such as nationalisation) or Soviet 'communism' (state capitalism). Here are a few examples:

> Socialism is defined by government ownership of the means of production with allocation and distribution by central planning, but with some reliance on the market when central planning gets overwhelmed (Daly and Cobb, 1989:13).

> ... I think greater clarity is achieved if we describe those societies in which the greater part of economic assets are not in formally private ownership as 'socialist' (however 'unsocialist' their institutions and practices may seem in other respects (Pierson, 1995:65).

> Generally speaking, socialism is in crisis because it bought secure but meager lives at the expense of freedom; but capitalism is in crisis because it has bought a prosperous freedom for some at the expense of security and community for all. Socialism suffers from scarcity, while capitalism suffers from overconsumption (Halal, 1996:235).

Halal's criticism of capitalism is welcome, but 'overconsumption' is surely not its major fault; his reference to socialist 'scarcity' can only be to Soviet-style state capitalism. Walzer (1983:318) has some specific ideas about what socialism is, some of which sound quite nice while others are definitely nasty. He advocates a decentralized democratic socialism; a strong welfare state run, in part at least, by local and amateur officials; a constrained market; an open and demystified civil service; independent public schools; the sharing of hard work and free time; the protection of religious and familial life; a system of public honouring and dishonouring free from all considerations of rank or class; workers' control of companies and factories; a politics of parties, movements, meetings and public debate.

White (1983:3) draws attention to the ways in which tyrannical leaders in the Third World have used 'socialism' for their own purposes: 'Rather than a force for international working class solidarity among the advanced capitalist nations, [socialism] has become a vehicle for radical nationalism in non-industrial societies.' Unfortunately his apparent belief that socialism has been a force for international working class solidarity is premature; the vast majority of members of the working class, supporting or at least acquiescing in capitalism as they now do, willingly line up behind their nationalistic leaders.

Finally, and perhaps king among the false friends of socialism, we have the buffoonery of George Bernard Shaw. With the quite undeserved reputation of being an intelligent socialist, Shaw wrote of socialism as 'a scheme for distributing wealth to everybody' (1971:46). He also made the ridiculous claim that 'socialism is from beginning to end a matter of law' (p.128). Whatever claims to fame Shaw may be thought to merit, being a true friend of socialism is not one of them.

Chapter 12

MARX ON SOCIALISM

Though Marx's critical analysis of capitalism is widely and rightly acclaimed, his contribution to describing what kind of society will replace it is sketchy. Partly because of his distrust of idealist utopias and partly because of his view of the unfolding of human history as a process, he famously refused to write recipes for future cookshops. Consequently his descriptions of future society are, as Avineri (1971:223) put it, 'most austere and restrained'. In the first part of this chapter we discuss the positive and revolutionary statements that Marx made about the nature of future socialist/communist society. In the second part we take a more critical view of the ways in which his attitude to the future society was influenced by reformist concerns and priorities.

His long view — truly revolutionary

Marx was not an idealist. For him (at least in the earlier stages of his writing) communism was a movement, not something to be established. This is how he and Engels described it:

> Communism is for us not a state of affairs which is to be established, an ideal to which reality will have to adjust itself. We call communism the real movement which abolishes the present state of things (1970:56).

According to Walker (1978:56) Marx 'saw socialism, not as some entirely new and radically different system, but as a 'transformed' version of capitalism, a social arrangement in which the methods and organization of exploitative society are put to a higher and humane purpose. Socialism is capitalism transcended.'

The conventional opinion about Marx's view of socialism/communism is that it consisted of two stages, sometimes called lower and higher or early and full. Moore (1993:67) argues that the socialism of the Communist Manifesto (the lower stage) is inconsistent with that of the Gotha Programme (the higher stage). But discussion of Marx's two stages of socialism may be an oversimplification. Buick (1978:152) maintains that Marx envisaged not two but three stages of socialism after the capture of political power by the working class:

1. A period during which the working class would use the political power it had just won to transform society from capitalism to communism.
2. A period immediately after the transfer of society from capitalism to communism when the new society would still bear some of the marks of the old but in which classes, the state, money and the wage system would have ceased to exist.
3. A period during which society would realise in full the communist ideal, which Marx called 'a higher phase of communist society'.

Leaving aside Buick's first and second stages, we may first examine the content of the third stage — the long-term goal, if you like — in Marx's own words. His description of full communism is couched very largely in philosophical — and even moral — terms rather than being an attempt to paint a picture (as Morris did) of 'how we shall live'. Thus in the Communist Manifesto he writes of the new society as being an 'association in which the free development of each is the condition for the free development of all' (Marx, 1977:238). He is also concerned with the sort of human nature that would be prevalent in the future communist society. In particular, Marx foresees communal creativity. With labour emancipated, every man becomes a working man:

> In communist society, where nobody has one exclusive sphere of activity but each can become accomplished in any branch he wishes, society regulates the general production and thus makes it possible for me to do one thing today and another tomorrow, to hunt in the morning, fish in the afternoon, rear cattle in the evening, criticise after dinner, just as I have a mind, without ever becoming hunter, fisherman, shepherd or critic (Marx, 1977:169).

Three of the four activities Marx chooses to illustrate the variety of tasks that people are likely to undertake and enjoy in a typical working day are rural rather than urban or industrial and the fourth (being a critic) can be done in any environment. This may be taken as a preference for country life over city life, a preference (as we shall see in the next chapter) even more keenly expressed by Morris. But Marx's concern is more philosophical than practical.

It is the principle of not being labelled or type-cast by what one does that he is trying to establish. He develops this point by reference to the difference between painting in capitalist and communist societies:

> ... with a communist organisation of society, there disappears the subordination of the artist to local and national narrowness, which arises entirely from division of labour, and also the subordination of the artist to some definite art, thanks to which he is exclusively a painter, sculptor, *etc.*, the very name of his activity adequately expressing the narrowness of his professional development and his dependence on division of labour. In a communist society there are no painters but at most people who engage in painting among other activities (Marx, 1977:189).

In his later writings (notably *The Critique of the Gotha Programme*) Marx seems to place less emphasis on what work in communist society will mean to people and more emphasis on the changes which will have to take place before full communism can be attained:

> In a higher phase of communist society, after the enslaving subordination of the individual to the division of labour, and therewith also the antithesis between mental and physical labour, has vanished; after labour has become not only a means of life but life's prime want; after the productive forces have also increased with the all-round development of the individual, and all the springs of co-operative wealth flow more abundantly — only then can the narrow horizon of bourgeois right be crossed in its entirety and society inscribe on its banners: From each according to his ability, to each according to his needs! (Marx, 1977:566).

The ending of restrictive division of labour is part of the revolutionary process, but so is the development of productive forces (much increased since Marx's time) and the wider use of co-operative methods. The give and take of abilities and needs, unmediated by property relations and money, is the goal.

Apart from work and the organisation of production, Marx ventured observations on education and the abolition of differences between town and country in communism. The Communist Manifesto includes these passages:

> The young folk as they pass through the schools will be taught the whole system of production as part of their education, they will be in a position to pass from one branch of industry to another according as social needs require or as their own inclinations impel... Thus a communistically organised society will be able to provide opportunities for the cultivation of all-round capacities (p.335).

> ... the erection of palatial dwellings on the natural domains where communities of citizens shall live together for the carrying on of industry and agriculture; where the advantages of town life shall be linked with those of country life without having to suffer from the one-sidedness and disadvantages of either (p.332).

The reconciliation of country and town life is a theme popular among later socialists, but exactly what Marx had in mind by 'palatial dwellings' is more questionable. Also his view of education, focused as it is on work and production, can hardly be said to be 'for life'. However, such speculations were rare for Marx and come close to writing recipes for future cookshops. They were probably made with the intention of putting a populist gloss on abstract ideas. Clearly he felt more comfortable with expounding theory:

> [Communism] is the genuine solution of the antagonism between man and nature and between man and man. It is the true solution of the struggle between existence and essence, between objectification and self-affirmation, between freedom and necessity, between individual and species (Marx, 1977:89).

This dialectical process of reconciling opposites, of creating a new synthesis out of the clash of thesis and antithesis, is at the heart of Marxism. It also helps to explain Marx's caution about predicting the future other than in terms of general principles. Modern interpreters of Marx do not always do him justice, but Fetscher's (1961) commentary seems justified:

> Inasmuch as they become changed people, so changed circumstances arise; and inasmuch as they create new circumstances so do they become new people... in human society nature becomes humanised at the same time as man becomes naturalised. This means that his humanity has become for him the whole of nature; nature is no longer alien to him but has become, through human activity and investigation, something intimate and close (pp.107–9).

His short view — unfortunate compromise

The second section of *The Communist Manifesto* includes a list of ten measures to be put into effect by the workers' parties immediately after their victory over the capitalists. It is not suggested that the measures describe features of the new society — rather, they are a tactic intended to gain support for the revolution. Marx (quoted in Ollman, 1977:10), in a discussion with the anarchist Bakunin, makes this clear: '... the proletariat must take measures, as a government, through which the peasant finds his position directly improved, which thus wins him for the revolution... These reformist measures are:

1. Abolition of property in land and application of all rents of land to public purposes
2. A heavy progressive or graduated income tax
3. Abolition of all right of inheritance
4. Confiscation of the property of all emigrants and rebels
5. Centralisation of credit in the hands of the state, by means of a national bank with state capital and an exclusive monopoly
6. Centralisation of the means of communication and transport in the hands of the state
7. Extension of factories and instruments of production owned by the state; the bringing into cultivation of waste-lands, and the improvement of the soil generally in accordance with a common plan
8. Equal liability of all to labour. Establishment of industrial armies, especially for agriculture
9. Combination of agriculture with manufacturing industries; gradual abolition of the distinction between town and country, by a more equable distribution of the population over the country
10. Free education for all children in public schools. Abolition of children's factory labour in its present form. Combination of education with industrial production, *etc*., *etc*.'

Perhaps the most striking thing about this list of 'immediate demands' is how similar many of them are to those put forward subsequently by the Soviet Communist Party and the bolder elements among Old Labour. It is not necessary to comment on them all, but some observations may serve to show how far Marx was prepared to go to advocate reforms of capitalism in the belief that they would somehow 'win people for the revolution':

- 'Confiscation... rebels.' This may be interpreted as a warning to the bourgeoisie not to engage in counter-revolutionary activity. The implication is that the proletariat's victory is not completed with the revolution but must expect opposition, even violent opposition. Ollman (1977:12) seeks to praise

Marx's 'humanity': 'It is indicative of the humanity with which Marx confronts counter-revolutionaries that confiscation is the most severe punishment ever mentioned.' Confiscation without the back-up of armed force?

- 'Centralisation... state.' Specifying that communication and transport are to be taken over by the state' suggests that most industries are not.
- 'Combination... country.' For Marx peasants are a 'class of barbarians' whose way of existence he labels 'the idiocy of rural life'. He apparently believes that country people have more to gain from town life than town people have to gain from country life.
- 'Free... production.' Marx thus envisages the continuation of part-time child labour. In Capital, vol.1, he spells this out, favouring an education that 'will in the case of every child over a given age combine productive labour with instruction and gymnastics, not only as one of the methods of adding to the efficiency of production but as the only method of producing fully developed human beings' (p.484).

Even in his later writings Marx seems more concerned with forecasting what will happen in the early, transitional stages of communism than in the eventual. 'full' version. In *Critique of the Gotha Programme* he declares 'From each according to his ability, to each according to his needs!' but does not elaborate the thought. Though clearly referring to full communism, these words amount to little more than a very good slogan. By contrast, he develops his view of the economic arrangements pertaining in 'early' communism (when it is 'still stamped with the birth marks of the old society from whose womb it emerged') at some length:

> ... the individual producer receives back from society — after the deductions have been made — exactly what he gives to it. What he has given to it is his individual quantum of labour. For example, the social working day consists of the sum of the individual hours of work; the individual labour time of the individual producer is the part of the social working day contributed by him, his share in it. He receives a certificate from society that he has furnished such and such an amount of labour (after deducting his labour for the common funds), and with this certificate he draws from the social stock of means of consumption as much as costs the same amount of labour. The same amount of labour which he has given to society in one form he receives back in another (Marx, 1977:568).

In short, to each according to his *work*, not his needs. A clumsy and bureaucratic alleged step on the road to full communism. No wonder that critics have questioned this reformist streak in Marx's thought. Thus Beilharz (2000:61) detects what he calls 'a slide into economism and grey industrialism' in some of Marx's writing. Socialism is centred on, and so reduced to, economy or 'necessity'. But early Marxism, sometimes dismissed as idealist, sought to question the whole idea of economy, not to harness it doubtfully for socialist ends, but to transform it certainly for those ends.

It may also be argued that Marx, particularly in his later writings, made too rigid a bifurcation between necessity and freedom, between work and leisure (Carter,1988:14). This from vol.3 of *Capital*:

> Freedom... can consist only in this, that socialized man, the associated producers, govern the human metabolism with nature in a rational way, bringing it under their collective control instead of being dominated by it as a blind power; accomplishing it with the least expenditure of energy and in conditions most worthy and appropriate for their human nature. But this always remains a realm of necessity. The true realm of freedom, the development of human powers as an end in itself, begins beyond it, though it can only flourish with this realm of necessity as its basis. The reduction of the working day is the basic prerequisite.

The two key phrases betraying Marx's concern with reforming capitalism in the direction of socialism, rather than with the building of socialism itself, are 'the least expenditure of energy' and 'reduction of the working day'. While in socialism people may well want to expend as little energy as possible on some tasks (such as 'dirty work'), this does not mean that they will also try to save energy on pleasant and creative work. Similarly with reduction of the working day. With capitalism, labour is sold in a competitive market and the work that has to be done for a wage or salary is often something to minimise. With socialism, enhancement of the working day — improving its quality — will surely be the aim.

Chapter 13

MORRIS ON SOCIALISM

William Morris, like Karl Marx, was concerned to offer a description of the society that both believed would and should replace capitalism. Marx, as we have seen, wrote of the future in largely theoretical terms, refusing to 'write recipes for future cookshops'. By contrast, Morris, although he knew of Marx's writings, contributed relatively little to socialist theory. Instead his preferred method, principally in *News from Nowhere*, but also to some extent in *A Dream of John Ball*, was to paint a picture of what a post-capitalist world would be like to live in.

Morris was a socialist for only the last thirteen years of his life, although during that relatively brief period he crammed in a remarkable amount of writing and public speaking. His views on how, in general terms, socialism would differ from capitalism are scattered throughout his later writings. The following, from his pamphlet 'How I became a socialist', sums up some of the main points:

> ... what I mean by Socialism is a condition of society in which there should be neither rich nor poor, neither master nor master's man, neither idle nor overworked, neither brain-sick brain workers nor heart-sick hand workers, in a word, in which all men would be living in equality of condition and would manage their affairs unwastefully, and with the full consciousness that harm to one would mean harm to all — the realization at last of the meaning of the word COMMONWEALTH (Morris, 1962:33).

This description of socialism is good as far as it goes, but I believe that it doesn't go far enough. It is strong on equality, the abolition of social classes and the reconciliation of hand and brain work. But it is weak on spelling out other vital aspects of socialism such as common ownership of the means of wealth production and distribution and how the replacement of government of persons by administration of things (democratic control) will be achieved. Something similar may be said about *News from Nowhere* — it paints some features of social life in more detail than others. But the picture is one of a whole living society, no matter that some detail is taken for granted, or perhaps just left for the people at the time to decide.

A vision more than a dream

In *News from Nowhere* Morris gives us his vision of what socialism will be like. Writing more than a century ago, he attempts to predict how life will be lived in the early 22nd century. He calls his futuristic tale a vision rather than a dream, but it is unavoidably a vision that takes no account of the tremendous changes that were to take place in the capitalist world during the 20th century. Morris makes no secret of his hatred of 19th century industrialism and his preference for the work methods, artefacts and life style typical of at least some of the people in the 14th century. As Hodgson (1987:128) observes, *Nowhere* is a vision of the future that consistently refers back to the past, whether of memory or history, and seeks to unite it with the future.

In *Nowhere* what I shall discuss in chapters 15–18 as the four central themes of socialism are illustrated, some at greater length than others. Taking the various incidents and situations in the order in which they occur in the book, they include:

Common ownership. Morris (through his main character William Guest) says relatively little about the form(s) that common ownership will take, and how it will differ in practice from capitalist private and state ownership. In the chapter 'Concerning government' he refers to the disappearance of the rights of property 'which mean the clenching the fist on a piece of goods and crying out to the neighbours You shan't have this!' We are left to guess how it is decided who shall have the use of such things as houses and gardens, although Morris does suggest that today's privately-owned 'stately homes' will have been converted into museums to which the public would have free access.

Democratic control. Morris has much more to say about how society and social processes will be organised and controlled. Central government has no place in Morris's future society: the Houses of Parliament, still preserved as a building, are 'a storage place for manure'. But he is no anarchist — in *Nowhere* parliament is not abolished but transformed: 'the whole people is our parliament'. Crime is much reduced because the private property basis for much of it has been removed.

Transgressions against 'good fellowship' (by which Morris presumably means anti-social actions) are treated as 'the errors of friends, not the habitual actions of persons driven into enmity against society'. There is no civil law or criminal law, and no prisons. Instead 'when any violence is committed, we expect the transgressor to make any atonement possible to him, and he himself expects it'. In the rare cases when the ill-doer is sick or mad 'he must be restrained till his sickness or madness is cured'.

Morris goes into considerable detail about how decisions will be taken which affect substantial numbers of people. His twin principles are decision by majority (vote) preceded by full discussion of all relevant considerations. The 'unit of management' is the commune, which has motes (periodic meetings of neighbours). Some decisions are simple and quick: 'a neighbour proposes a change, and of course if everybody agrees there is an end of discussion, except about details.' But if the matter goes to a vote, and the vote is close, 'the question is again put off for further discussion'. It may even go to a third meeting, seeking to avoid what Morris calls 'the wound caused by the tyranny of a majority'. He clearly recognises the problem of reconciling a desirable degree of democracy with a reasonable degree of efficiency.

Production for use. Right from the outset of his journey into the future, Guest is made aware that people do and make things simply because they are needed, not because of wages or profit-seeking. The Thames boatman offers Guest his services as a guide, not for reward but because he has a week to spare. Work — pleasant, creative, not forced or excessive — is sometimes in short supply: a friend is said to be 'on the look-out for a stroke of work'. Instead of factories there are Banded-workshops, 'places where people collect who want to work together'. Morris (through Guest) shows how work has become integrated with leisure. He comes across a gang of men road mending, laughing and talking as they worked, 'looking much like a boating party at Oxford would have looked in the days I remembered'. In *Nowhere* 'men make for their neighbours' use as if they were making for themselves, not for a vague market of which they know nothing, and over which they have no control... Nothing can be made except for genuine use; therefore no inferior goods are made.'

Free access. There are many illustrations in *Nowhere* of the way in which people have free access to what they need instead of being denied because of lack of money. Guest's boatman is puzzled when asked 'how much? — he would offer his services freely to anybody. There are no poor people (and of course no rich) except in the sense of those in poor health. There is talk of shopping, but apparently only to go to places where one can pick up what is needed: 'the people were ignorant of the arts of buying and selling'. When Guest is worried about losing his pipe he is told 'What will it matter if you do? Somebody is sure to find it, and he will use it, and you can get another.' Even with larger items such as houses, the principle is to allocate according to need. Referring to the early stages of socialism, we learn that 'people from the cleared slums took [former business premises] for lodgings and dwelt there'.

More than a century after his death, the work of William Morris continues to attract attention and admiration. A flourishing William Morris Society perpetuates the tremendous variety of his work, of which advocating socialism was only part (though, so far as this book is concerned, the most important part). Some of the tributes to Morris are, to put it kindly, on the saccharine side. Thus for Hodgson (1987:124) he was 'a fighter for freedom and a good life for all'. But other commentators make more substantial points, and provoke us to think more about the nature of Morris's contribution to the development of socialist thought and future practice.

The historian A.L Morton believes that Morris 'was a man passionately in love with the classless society, determined to seek and ensure it by all possible means: it was in Marxism that he found the road...'(1952:163). Morton further identifies Morris as author of one of the great English utopias. Rather than being a state of ideal perfection which can never be achieved and hence can be dismissed as impracticable, Morton suggests that utopias such as Morris's can play a useful role in transforming society:

> ... the essence of the classical utopias of the past was a belief that by satire, by criticism or by holding up an example to be followed, they could help to change the world. In this they have had a positive part to play, they have stimulated thought, led men to criticise and fight against abuses, taught them that poverty and oppression were not a part of a natural order of things which must be endured (p.212).

Meier (1978:53) agrees with Morton that the main inspiration and starting point of Morris's utopia is to be sought in Marxism. He also makes the point that Morris places work at the heart of existence:

> If, in capitalist society, it had become a sordid chore, the first task of communism would be to make it once more a need and a joy, by way of diversity of occupation and man's expression of himself through his work (p.84).

Utopia does not always get a uniformly good press, but Coleman and O'Sullivan (1990:9) speak well of it in connection with Morris's work: 'The utopian imagination, at its most radical, invades the prevailing concept of reality, undermines certainties about what humans must always be like, and casts doubt upon the inevitability of the relations of everyday life.' More recently Coleman (1996:*vi*), a keen interpreter and advocate of Morris's ideas, has drawn attention to the ethical dimension of utopian ideas which contain, but go far beyond, conventional politics:

> For Morris and his comrades politics was about the making of history, by the many and in accordance with an ethical design more ambitious than any yet conceived or attempted.

Some criticisms of the vision

Much of what Morris describes in *Nowhere* has no direct connection with the fundamentals of socialism (common ownership, democratic control, production for use and free access). Pleasant though most of the descriptions are, they are not helpful, and certainly are not essential to the case for socialism. Morris makes no secret of his admiration for life in the 14th century. Fulsome descriptions abound of the beautiful clothing and adornments of both men and women. Conceding that shoddiness and poor workmanship and materials would be inconsistent with the socialism Morris seeks to portray, it is not self-evident that 14th century customs and fashions are aesthetically more pleasing than, say, the simple, futuristic clothes worn by Star Trek characters.

Morris's preference for country in his town-country 'integration', his defence of women's work and men's work, and his rejection of schools as a feature of education are also open to question. We can never know the answer to the purely hypothetical question of whether Morris would have reacted to early 21st century industrialism as he did to the 19th century variety. His views of man-woman relationships and division of labour were arguably 'progressive' in his day — today they smack more of the traditional, if not the reactionary. And, given that some of his criticism of the role of schools in education is justified, it by no means follows that developments in educational ideas and school practices are without merit.

Some claims about Morris's future socialist world are unfounded. For example, Green and Sutcliffe (1987:376) believe that in *Nowhere* 'the near-complete absence of conflict and the permanent joy of his characters are both cloying and unconvincing'. While it is true that class conflict and war have been abolished, conflict in the milder sense of disagreement between individuals and groups is certainly not unknown or even rare, as with the 'obstinate refusers' who insist on finishing their own work before joining in the harvest gathering. Morris does not describe his characters as having lives of 'permanent joy'. Even in a society that doesn't risk life and limb in pursuit of profit, accidents do happen. Thus on one occasion 'a mishap... cost the lives of two men and a woman'.

A more serious criticism of Morris's view of socialism is his assumption that when it is presented to people as a practical alternative to capitalism they will respond readily and positively. The historian E. P. Thompson (1977:334) takes up this theme when referring to Morris as one of the pioneers of revolutionary socialism: 'So clear and simple did the matter appear to some of the pioneers that it seemed only necessary to go to the street-cars and explain it to the workers, and they would be ready to rise.' Thompson also quotes from a letter by Morris about the coming of the international proletarian revolt:

> In all probability England will go first — will give the signal, though she is at present so backward: Germany, with her 700,000 Socialists, is pretty nearly ready; France, sick of her republic of stock-jobbers and pirates, is nearly as far on... (p.335).

Such completely unfounded optimism about the coming of socialism was rife at the end of the 19th century. It was based partly on a belief that the socialist message, once broadcast, would be readily accepted by workers but also on a physical rather than an intellectual concept of the campaign: a revolt or a rising rather than a propagandist exercise or an educational campaign. This is reflected in Morris's long chapter in *Nowhere* on 'How the change came'.

The sequence of events he foresaw was: growing discontent among the workers; met by minimum wage legislation, price controls and government factories (collectively and unfortunately called 'State socialism' by Morris); the demand of the Combined Workers to acquire the means of wealth production and distribution; a public meeting in Trafalgar Square resulting in death and imprisonment of some protesters; the formation of a workers' Committee of Public Safety; 'unorganised pillage' of big shops; a state of siege proclaimed by the government; followed by riots in several cities; a further big meeting in Trafalgar Square at which the crowd were machine-gunned by the army, resulting in 1,000-2,000 deaths; support for the government repressive action by even the 'liberal' press; the call by one brave editor to withdraw the state of siege and arrest the soldiers for murder; widespread public support for the editor; the government making 'a show of yielding to the demands of the people'; the imprisonment of the Committee of Public Safety; a general strike; the discharge of the prisoners; a brief and unsuccessful armed campaign by counter-revolutionaries; and 'at last it became clear to all men that the cause which was once hopeless was now triumphant'.

Bizarre and anachronistic though this projected sequence of events must seem to socialists and non-socialists alike at the beginning of the 21st century, we must appreciate that for someone writing in 1890 it would not have seemed so unlikely. In 1887, only three years before Morris was writing *Nowhere*, a protest meeting in Trafalgar Square had led to violence, though not on the scale of the worst he predicted.

Morris refers ambiguously to the role of education as part of the change ('educational articles.. admirable and straightforward expressions of the doctrines and practice of Socialism') but gives no indication of what happens to make most workers become socialists so quickly. The whole sequence of events predicted by Morris is essentially *political* rather than educational — heavily dependent on the actions of leaders, committees, police and armed forces — which contrasts oddly with Guest being told in the 11-line chapter 'Concerning politics' that 'we are very well off as to politics — because we have none'.

Chapter 14

REVOLUTION, NOT REFORMISM

Both reformism and revolution involve change. With reformism the change sought is superficial, the intention being to amend the system in one or a few small ways, but to leave it basically intact. With revolution the change sought is fundamental; one basic system is to be replaced by another. There are two kinds of reformism. One has no intention of revolution — indeed it may use reforms to *oppose* revolution. The other cherishes the mistaken belief that successful reforms will somehow prepare the ground for revolution — such reforms are seen as first steps on the long road to revolution.

In this chapter we first consider how reformers today persuade themselves and others that modest and achievable changes (not revolution) are what is generally wanted. Against this there is evidence of the futility of reformism, at least from a revolutionary point of view. Thirdly, the slow progress — and in numerical terms the failure — of 'the left' to achieve more than superficial reforms is wrongly blamed on its 'disunity'. Then we discuss the question on the lips of many reformers, including those who have given up on revolution (they probably didn't really want it in the first place): 'What kind of capitalism should we support?' Finally, we outline the positive case for revolutionary change from capitalism to socialism.

Reforming capitalism

Reformism has some attractions over revolution — especially if you are unimaginative, don't like confrontation, prefer to think in the short term, and don't want to be accused of not living in 'the real world'. You are also assured of being in good company — large numbers of people think (or fail to think) as you do. Social scientists describe this situation and comment on it — usually favourably. Thus Peet (1991:182): 'There are billions of peasants, workers, students and intellectuals who want, expect and are prepared to struggle for a form of development organized to transform the lives of the masses'. Well, yes, there probably are, but the 'struggle' isn't very determined except in a very few cases, and is usually limited to improving material standards of living within capitalism. Brenner (1984:5) makes a similar point, but for some unexplained reason he uses the past tense instead of the present:

> Members of the working class strove to protect and improve their living standards and share in the rising affluence the system was producing. They did not reject capitalist utilitarianism, but affirmed it, in the belief that their material needs and social security could best be served by collective efforts in trade unions or political parties.

As Brenner observes, reforms are promoted by trade unions and political parties. It is possible to have a political party that does not advocate reforms, but in practice nearly all of them do. Trade unions (which are often linked to reformist political parties) have generally been declining in numbers and influence in advanced industrial countries, mainly because of the policies of economic 'liberalism'. Trade union leaders and spokespeople insist that workers express a need for representation, for a collective voice in the workplace. Green (2000:280) advocates what he calls social-movement unionism, as opposed to business unionism. He believes that workers can and should assert 'new rights as citizens and workers, as brothers and sisters determined to defend the dignity and security of wage-earning families.'

It has been, is, and will be an uphill battle for workers, with very little achieved for all the effort. Capitalism is marginally better with trade unions than without them, just as it is marginally better with income support systems, progressive income tax, winter fuel payments for the elderly, and the myriad other reforms that are offered to workers to sweeten the pill of exploitation. Historically there has been a loose connection between trade unionism and socialism, but when it comes to the crunch trade unions are on the side of capitalism. The union leader John L. Lewis recognised this and was unusually frank about it: 'Trade unionism is a phenomenon of capitalism quite similar to the corporation. One is essentially a pooling of labour for the purpose of common action in production and sales. The other is a pooling of capital for exactly the same purpose. The economic aims of both are identical — gain' (quoted in Moody, 1988:57).

The futility of reformism

Reformism isn't a futile activity for everybody — it is a most excellent strategy if you want only small changes in a society that you are basically happy with. However, reformism is futile for two other categories of people: those who believe that capitalism can be reformed so that it operates in the interests of the majority, and those who expect that a programme of reforms will 'win the workers for the revolution' and hence be a contribution to the achievement of socialism.

The idea that capitalism can be humanised and changed by a series of reform measures is nearly as old as the capitalist system itself (Perrin, 2000:22). But reforms are implemented by political parties that seek and get a mandate to run capitalism. The motives for reforms may include an anxiety to relieve suffering and keenness to promote well-being, but the measures have the effect of serving the system rather then meeting the needs of individuals or groups.

Examples of reforms serving capitalism over the last two centuries are not hard to find. The Poor Law of 1834 was a response to mass destitution as peasants were driven off the land — the resulting crime and poor health (and hence poor productivity) of the workers were expensive to the ruling class. The post-1945 Welfare State introduced measures of health and social security intended to raise workers' efficiency and thus make them more productive of profit for the capitalist class — poverty was re-organised, not abolished.

The role of hegemony — conventional education, the media, a culture of consumption (see chapter 9) — is important in understanding why reformism as a policy fails to result in substantially improving the living conditions of the majority of people. The hard work of devising schemes for reforms, mounting campaigns in support of them, meeting opposition to them, eventually implementing them, is not the responsibility of members of the capitalist class (though they may give some of their wealth to promoting reforms they like). The main responsibility for reforms is undertaken by workers, that is, the roughly 98 percent of the population who are not capitalists). Furthermore, one person's advocated reform is sometimes another person's status quo. To Old Labour, nationalisation was a reform; to New Labour at least some privatisations are reforms.

Another objection to reformism is its essentially limited and short-term nature, Coleman (1996) likens a programme of reforms to attacking a tiger one claw at a time, and he goes on to describe the result as being 'so immersed in the expediencies of immediate palliation that one loses sight of any other end than a patched-up present' (p.*xxviii*). Another animal analogy is used by Lam (1996:255): campaigns for reforms are 'something akin to Jonah's struggle from inside the belly of the whale'. At present we are all entrapped inside capitalism. Our critiques of it spring necessarily from a place of containment. Reforms appear to be the easy answer to such containment, but still leave us within the belly of the beast.

The blind alley of 'left' unity

Political parties and policies are often divided into left, right and centre, sometimes with finer gradations such as centre left, centre right, far left and far right. Revolutionaries don't seek to be given any of these labels, but are often put in with the far left. Reformers can be found anywhere along the spectrum, though more likely on the left than the right.

The kind of reformers who believe they are taking the first steps on the long road to revolution look for quick results — so they want as many people as possible to support their proposals for reform. Reformers say to revolutionaries 'You are splitting the left. We are all working for the same goal, so why don't you join us? We can get strength through unity!'

Revolutionaries must reject this appeal if they are to remain revolutionaries. Reformism is never a contribution to the achievement of socialism — it is a diversion of energies from that goal. The offer of unity proposed by the reformer to the revolutionary is always a poisoned chalice: 'Join us today to promote (small but achievable reform) and tomorrow we'll start the revolution together.' But of course tomorrow never comes.

Another line of thinking that presents itself as friendly to revolution but is really calculated to frustrate it is 'the time is not yet ripe' argument. Consider this statement by Biel (2000:322):

> The organised left has itself opted for a mode of action which downplays (without completely abandoning) the idea of directly challenging the system... The left has had to retreat *for a time* from organising an alternative political economy, and is working instead on the terrain of capitalism (my emphasis).

'Working on the terrain of capitalism' is a euphemism for working for reforms. There are two implications in what Biel is saying. One is that there was a time when the left — or at least part of it — was working for revolutionary change (socialism). The other is that, since the retreat was only 'for a time', there would be a time in the future when working for socialism would come to the top of the agenda instead of being 'downplayed'. A further interesting question is why the left 'has had to retreat' from something that it never really did anyway, *i.e.* work wholeheartedly for socialism. Were the arguments for capitalism so strong that its opponents were forced into retreat? More likely those reformers who said they were willing to be revolutionaries in the long term succumbed to the status-quo-preserving goodies that they saw within their grasp.

What kind of capitalism to support?

As we saw in chapter 9, the forces supporting capitalism — conventional education, the media, hegemony and a culture of consumption — are strong and pervasive. Their combined message to would-be revolutionaries is 'Don't even *think* about changing the system. Better still, don't even think there *is* a system.' With alternatives ruled out, with ice-cream the only food on offer, the question becomes: what flavour do you want?

The death of socialism has often been proclaimed but on closer inspection it turns out to be the wrong body — that of Labour nationalisation, Soviet state capitalism, or something else. However, no chances are taken on resurrection or revolutionary life persisting somewhere. So a major task of opponents of revolutionary change is to convince us that revolution is impossible.

One argument against revolution is that it can't succeed quickly and because it can't succeed quickly it is better not to support it from the start. It is, of course, a circular argument, a negative self-fulfilling prophecy. Shutt (1999) and Heilbroner (1992) put it in slightly different ways. First Shutt:

> Attempts to replace one system *instantaneously* with a quite different one will always fail... any suggestion that we can or should seek to evolve a more viable economic order in its place will be dismissed as inherently utopian... any suggestion that the status quo will need to undergo fundamental adjustment is bound to be portrayed as eccentric (p.229, my emphasis).

From that quotation you may wish to give Shutt the benefit of the doubt — perhaps he is deploring the situation he is describing. Wrong! Elsewhere he advocates reforms that 'severely downgrade' profit maximisation (p.218), that increase and diversify consultation of the electorate (p.220), and that discriminate in favour of the most disadvantaged areas (p.223).

Then Heilbroner:

> The transition is too difficult, the rearrangements too complex, and above all, the opposition too ferocious for any such truly revolutionary change to occur in so short a time, historically speaking (p.118).

Some revolutions may approach being instantaneous, for example, an ignorant and supine mass offers no resistance when a new dictatorship replaces an old one. But the socialist revolution is not a change in who runs the system — it is a fundamental change of the system itself, which can only be made when the ideas supporting it are held by the population at large. Actually, Shutt's use of the phrase 'seek to evolve' is not out of place; although it implies a gradual change, that is what will happen. The revolutionary movement will grow as more and more people understand and support it. 'Utopian' and 'eccentric' are adjectives used by those who oppose the revolution or don't think that it is possible — which amounts to the same thing.

Heilbroner also relies on 'so short a time' as a deterrent to embarking on the revolutionary journey. Certainly the transition won't be easy, the rearrangements will be complex, and we must expect opposition. But those considerations shouldn't deter us from starting the process, if we can see that at the end of it we shall have achieved something worthwhile.

At present the revolutionary socialist movement is weak. It is kept from being stronger by those who claim there is no alternative to capitalism so we must concentrate on which kind we will support, or at least settle for. This from the Labour MP Denis MacShane: 'For years socialists used to argue about what kind of socialism we wanted... The choice of the left is no longer what kind of socialism it wants, but what kind of capitalism it can support.' (quoted in Greider,1997:36). The arguments about 'what kind of socialism we wanted' could not have been very inspirational — probably they were arguments about just another set of reforms of capitalism.

The journal *New Statesman* offers general support to New Labour's reforms, but to describe that support as lukewarm would be to vastly exaggerate the heat. Its editorial of 25 September 1998 is worth quoting at length:

> The arguments for electing Labour governments have never been based wholly, or even mainly, on the likelihood of their bringing about equality or the abolition of poverty or any of the other traditional aims of social democracy. Within two or three years of taking office, Labour, more often than not, is blown off course and forced to introduce policies quite at variance with its original intentions, slashing, for example, the public services on which the poor depend. But Labour governments have usually nudged things in the right direction. The economic gains for the poor folk of Barnsley,

Blackburn or Bootle may be scarcely measurable at the end of a period of Labour government but at least, for a year or two, their voices have counted in Whitehall and Westminster and, with luck, their children will be taught in slightly smaller classes or their local bus services will run a little bit more frequently or their hospitals will be a little less dilapidated.

But, looking at New Labour's achievements so far in its second term of office, don't bank on even those small mercies. Such are the achievements of a reforming party, proud not to be revolutionary. It is not for nothing that chapter 2 of Morrison's (2001) book on *New Labour* is titled 'The status quo party'. Thank goodness a party was not elected that nudged things in the *wrong* direction!

We must oppose the system

Marx and Morris clearly understood that revolution, not reformism, is the socialist goal. Another 19th century revolutionary, Rosa Luxemburg, attacked what she called revisionism:

> If we follow the political conception of revisionism... Our programme becomes not the realisation of socialism but the reform of capitalism; not the suppression of the system of wage labour, but the diminution of exploitation, that is, the suppression of the abuses of capitalism instead of the suppression of capitalism itself (quoted in Wright, 1986:65).

Capitalism, like an old car, has developed many faults and always seems to be needing costly repairs and new parts. Isn't it about time we scrapped it and got a new one? The analogy isn't a particularly good one — for one thing, replacing cars costs only money, while replacing social systems takes much thought and organisation — but at least it reminds us that things (whether cars or social systems) don't have to be patched up for ever.

The number of writers willing to state clearly that they support revolutionary change here and now is unfortunately small. A few were mentioned in chapter 6. Even those who do, tend to stress opposition to the old system rather than support of the new. Thus Dawson and Foster (1998:64), whose main subject is communications:

> The critique of existing communications must reach beyond a shallow critique of commercialization and extend to monopoly capital and the global system itself. Above all, it must be realized that nothing can be won, nothing of any value saved, except by opposing the system itself.

Bahro (1982), whose main concern is environmentalism, does link it with a wider social revolution:

> ... the ecology crisis will force us to say goodbye to capitalism... We must learn that socialism cannot be the continuation of this industrial system, it must involve a break with it (pp.62, 129).

These general statements appear to offer the promise of revolution, but they are deceptive. Elsewhere Bahro writes of 'reforms with a revolutionary content... reforms of a major and system-transcending kind' (p.44) but we are not given examples at that point. Later he writes approvingly of boycotting elections, obstructing the building of nuclear power stations, refusing to pay taxes, *etc*. (p.155). Slight wounding of capitalism, maybe. Construction of socialism, certainly not.

The destruction of capitalism without the building of a social system to take its place is conceivable but hardly sensible. Before discussing the future of capitalism in the final chapter, we need to clarify in what ways it is likely to be fundamentally different from capitalism, while possible to be initially constructed within capitalism. This we shall do in the next four chapters.

Chapter 15

COMMON OWNERSHIP

Capitalism	*Socialism*
Private or state ownership	Common ownership (no ownership)
Basically two classes (owners and non-owners of the means of wealth production)	All people equal control and access to means of production
Nation states, wars, armed and police forces	No nation states, wars, armed and police forces
Crime (mostly property), a legal system to uphold property rights	No property crime, any residual crime dealt with humanely

In this and the next three chapters I shall outline what I believe are likely to be the main features of a future socialist world which will distinguish it from capitalism. As long as the majority of the population support, or at least acquiesce in, the continuation of some form of capitalism, it is not possible to have 'actually existing socialism'. The most that can be claimed is that within capitalism there are some indications — limited foretastes, if you like — of what living in a socialist world will be like. Thus, for instance, we can say that in socialism all things will be as free as the air we breathe. Sometimes the little 'socialism' we had is taken away from us; movements in the apparent direction of socialism are reversed. Centuries ago, former common land was enclosed. More recently, the 'free' teeth, *etc.* under the original National Health Service had charges imposed on them.

In a sense, both capitalism and socialism are indivisible. They are whole systems, the parts of which mutually support and reinforce each other. In this chapter we shall focus on questions concerned with ownership, but each question under that heading doesn't stand alone. Also, each of our three later concerns — focusing on production, control and access — are of a piece with questions of ownership. Developments away from capitalism and towards socialism cannot get far out of line with each other for any length of time. There is, in fact, so little socialism in the world today because there are so few socialists in the world today.

Common ownership

A fundamental difference between capitalism and socialism is in the ownership of the means of producing and distributing wealth. With capitalism such means can be privately owned in various ways (by individuals, partnerships, trusts, corporations, *etc.*), ownership can be vested in the state and administered by officials on behalf of the state, or a mixture of the two. Some 'wealth', for example, intellectual capital in the form of scientific knowledge, may not be owned by anybody, although venture capitalists are constantly seeking ways to bring such 'free' goods to the market by patenting them.

With socialism all that is in and on the earth will be commonly owned or, if you like, not owned by anybody. People may possess, or by common consent have exclusive or shared use of, certain goods and services. But there will be no title deeds or other 'evidence' of possession, and no law or armed force to protect and enforce possession. It is not inconceivable that there will be disputes about possession, but these are likely to be resolved by some form or mediation or arbitration (see chapter 17 on problems of control in socialism).

In socialism the extent to which goods and services are regarded as effectively 'owned' (kept and/or used by one individual or a small group such as a family) or owned by no one may be expected to vary from place to place and from time to time. The whole array of what in capitalism are known as capital and consumer goods, and services in the broadest sense of that term, may be grouped according to how personal or how public the various items are likely to be regarded:

1. Items for personal use, such as toothbrushes, spectacles, *etc.*). These will effectively be 'owned' by individuals, in some cases because they are specifically made for those individuals. The only difference from capitalism will be that the items are always made available according to need, not

bought, sold or exchanged. (Controversial question: will some people insist on having 100 pairs of shoes, and if so will they be indulged or discouraged?).

2. Items that can be used either by one person or by different people at different times. Examples are items of clothing or personal adornment, home furniture and furnishings, *etc*. The effective 'ownership' is most likely to be individual or familial, but can be shared over time . (Controversial question: in what circumstances may there still be secondhand clothes or furniture?)

3. The products of individual or small group work, such as paintings, sculptures, collections of various kinds, the produce of gardens and farms. The public at large will normally have access to such items, but they may sometimes be 'kept' by the makers, collectors or growers. (Controversial question: with some very rare or unique items, how will it be decided that they have a temporary or permanent resting place or travel from time to time and from place to place?)

4. Buildings of various kinds, chiefly for residential, work, educational, social, leisure and cultural purposes. People may expect to occupy small dwellings individually, in families or with a few friends with larger buildings for those who prefer to live more communally. Workplaces of various sizes and types may be combined with living accommodation or separate from it. 'Ownership' in the sense of making decisions about the construction and use of buildings will be in the hands of those who use or work in them (see chapter 17). (Controversial question: will we have 'motes', or something equivalent, to resolve competing claims for occupancy?)

5. The largest items, including what are now known as fixed capital, and natural resources: land, networks of transport, communication and education facilities, sites of special scientific or historical interest. Except perhaps for parcels of land, there appears to be no reason for these resources to be held other than in common, though the arrangements for their use will be more complex than with smaller items. (Controversial question: how to resolve conflicts between provision for public versus private means of transport?)

A classless society

All forms of capitalism are based on private or state ownership and control of the means of wealth production and distribution. Such ownership necessarily involves the existence of social classes. Apologists for capitalism like to distinguish several classes: upper, middle, working, lower — and perhaps finer categories such as upper-middle and lower-middle. This implies a gradation rather than a class division: you work your way up a class ladder instead of being on one side or the other of a class division.

However, capitalist reality is closer to a class struggle than a ladder of achievement. If you own enough wealth to be able to live comfortably without the need to find an employer, then you are in a small minority, perhaps two or three percent of the general population. The rest, the other 98 percent, have to find an employer, or live off the state or charity, or starve. Even if they are relatively highly paid, they have to accumulate a substantial amount of capital if they want to rise out of the working class. Of course, individuals may be lucky enough to inherit or win sufficient wealth to become capitalists. And workers are not necessarily employed — they may be unemployed, retired or the dependants of employees. Capitalism is, in short, best understood as a two-class system, despite some borderline cases and variations in income and wealth among the members of each class.

With socialism the word 'class' may still be used, but it won't denote how you stand regarding ownership of the means of wealth production and distribution — an owner or a non-owner. Instead, every man, woman and child will stand equally as regards such ownership. Privileged class membership entails substantial advantages in capitalism: a higher (sometimes a very much higher) material standard of living, better education, living in a healthier environment. having better access to costly medical services, and so on. But working-class members suffer the obverse: relative or absolute poverty, an inferior education, an unhealthy environment, poor or no access to health services. Such inequality will be eradicated in socialism — not entirely at first in all parts of the world, but the policy will be a genuine one of pursuing social equality and not a sham one of 'equal opportunity' as in class-divided capitalist society.

In the absence of divisive social class, there may well be non-divisive ways in which people may wish to identify themselves, and be identified, as members of a group. What you do, what you like doing, and are perhaps specially skilled or experienced at doing, may be a label you are happy to wear. Marx insisted that there would be no painters designated as such in socialism. Morris thought otherwise: his Boffin was a dustman, with none of the disadvantages that most dustmen have in capitalism — but he was apparently still happy to be called a dustman. It will be interesting to see how far people in socialism will want to be known by some designation linked with what they do or with some other criterion.

Socialism is sometimes said to mean a society of drab equality, of regimentation and loss of individual differences. I can see no good reason for this supposition. There won't be winners and losers in the class sense of capitalism, but why shouldn't there be some forms of competition and therefore some winners and losers with no exclusive privileges heaped on the winners and no dire consequences for the losers? A footrace in which the aim is for all competitors to finish in a straight line is not unthinkable, but doesn't seem very sensible.

Also there is the question of expertise. Capitalism loves people who excel at something: their celebrity performances (sporting, artistic or otherwise) attract big paying audiences and thus produce big profits for the few elite performers, their promoters, trainers, managers, *etc.* Sometimes the elite performer suffers a life unbalanced by over-concentration on getting to, and staying at, the top. I can't see this kind of expertise being encouraged in socialism, but why shouldn't some painters (in apparent defiance of Marx) devote a very large part of their lives to their artistic expression?

No nation states, no forces of repression

Some of the ugliest features of capitalism are its nation states, wars, armed and police forces. Socialism will have none of these. That need not mean the abolition of the positive side of recognising nations seen as different parts of the world that have different languages (though I guess the development of a universal language is likely, at least for some purposes), different national dishes, people with different physical and even psychological features according to where they were born. But it will mean the abolition of nationalism as a killer disease. Aggressive nationalism — there really is no other kind — requires armies to protect national borders or territory, preparations for war, periodic actual war.

With socialism boundaries between the territories of hostile and potentially hostile nation states will be a thing of the past. There will certainly need to be administrative boundaries of some kind, but these will be co-operative units, no more hostile to each other or unco-operative than, say, Surrey and Sussex are today (indeed, likely to be more co-operative than those counties are today).

Regardless of geographical location (island, region, continent or administrative area), people will regard themselves above all as citizens of the world. This will not stop them identifying with a part of the world in which they were born and brought up, or in which they have chosen to live, or which they prefer because it suits their tastes and interests better than any other place.

No property crime

With capitalism, crime is a big industry. It involves criminals, police forces, the judiciary, prisons, the probation service, criminologists, security personnel, safe deposits, locksmiths, neighbourhood watch schemes, and so on. Most, but not all, crime is connected with property — stealing things that 'belong' to someone else, with or without violence. Other crime does not involve property but is to do with breaking laws, including those enacted for the common good. To kill or injure someone is a crime — except when sanctioned by a government engaged in war. To commit an act of treason, not itself a violent act, may result in legalised violence (death in some countries) to the perpetrator.

Socialism won't see the end of all anti-social behaviour or occasional acts of violence, but it will certainly see the end of property-based crime. Anti-social behaviour today is often resorted to out of frustration. For instance, anger is often felt by people who are stimulated by advertising to consume costly goods and services but are not given legitimate access to money to buy them. In socialism there won't be any pressure to consume, no artificially stimulated wants, no 'shop till you drop' and no motive to steal. I agree with Morris that acts of murder will not be unknown but will be very rare and probably carried out by individuals who are temporarily and perhaps permanently insane. They will need to be restrained — and treated, not punished.

The consequences of anti-social behaviour will be very different in socialism from what they are in capitalism. In Morris's words, such behaviour will be treated as 'the errors of friends, not the habitual actions of persons driven into enmity against society'. It is reasonable to see a difference in the frequency of anti-social behaviour in the early stages of socialism as compared with the subsequent stages. With memories of late capitalism still lingering in the minds of some (particularly older) people, it may be that more actions will be seen as anti-social, and sterner deterrent measures taken against them, than when socialist norms and values will have been long established.

Punishment, revenge and retaliation will have no place in socialist society. However, there may well be differences in what is regarded as normal and what is regarded as deviant behaviour. Another and slightly different way of perceiving this difference is to suppose that, to some extent at least, individuals will continue to veer towards being either authoritarian or libertarian in their approach to social relations. It is perhaps a fundamental dilemma facing any society. To what extent is it important to have social order, to hold the society together, to defend it against anti-social actions? Equally important, how far should dissent from majority views be tolerated and even encouraged, alternatives to the status quo be freely discussed, and control of social processes be as relaxed as possible?

My own view (at present but not unamenable to change) is that the gap between socialists disposed to favour authority over liberty and those of the opposite persuasion will narrow as socialism is approached. Already it is fair to say that there are few, if any, control freaks or organisation-hating anarchists among socialists. I don't rule out the possibility that in different parts of the world there will be different resolutions of this dilemma — some places where you will find more emphasis on one set of norms and values than another. But the dialectical confrontation of thesis and antithesis — of order and change — will surely be with us as far as we can see into the future.

Chapter 16

PRODUCTION FOR USE

Capitalism	*Socialism*
Production for profit Employment (employers, employees, unemployed and retired)	Production to meet human needs Work (all those fit enough volunteer services as preferred and needed)
Mostly hierarchical organisation and communication (giving/taking orders)	Mostly lateral organisation and communication (agreed plan)
Mostly short and medium term perspective	Short, medium and long term perspective as appropriate

If the common theme of the matters discussed in the previous chapter was ownership, then the common theme in this chapter is production. We first consider what is implied by socialist production solely to meet human need and how it compares with capitalist production aimed primarily to make a profit. Then there is the question of capitalist employment (paid work for the majority) and socialist non-paid work (available to all). With no work needed which serves only to support the capitalist system, the range of work will be narrowed and its quality as a human experience enhanced. Emphasis on giving and taking orders will change to everyone working either informally or to a democratically agreed plan. Finally, long-term considerations will feature in all planning and decision making much more prominently than in capitalism.

Production for need, not profit

With capitalism the general motive for the production of goods and services is the pursuit of profit. All capitalist enterprise has to keep a constant and watchful eye on the 'bottom line' — how much profit. Goods and services are put on the market (offered for sale) only when there is prospect of profit. The question of meeting human need is not irrelevant to capitalism, but it is subservient to the pursuit of profit. Goods and services are designed to meet needs — or, rather, wants, including wants manufactured and stimulated by advertising. Nearly half the world's population stands in need of adequate food, shelter, health services, *etc.* but the market does not generally meet those needs except for payment (only a small part of total need is met by gifts or charity).

Capitalism prefers to satisfy wants rather than needs — wants are virtually unlimited and because they are expressed through economic demand there is more profit in meeting them. In 'rich' countries a market can be created for waterproof bible covers or doll-like working models of actual children. Elsewhere children in families with no money are left to starve to death. Some capitalist institutions, instead of being in the market, are designed to serve the market system. Taxes of various kinds enable the state and government apparatus to be financed. Such 'production' meets the needs of the system. So capitalism attaches greater importance to meeting them than to the more basic needs of its citizens. The provider-customer nexus overrides that of the provider-citizen.

With socialism, some needs will remain universal, but may be met in different ways according to climate. location, availability of natural resources, individual or group preferences. To take food as an example, its satisfaction as a need will no doubt vary from place to place and from time to time. Some people will feel a need to be vegetarians of varying degrees of strictness, others will be content to eat meat as part of their diet. There may well be different ratios of fresh to processed food. Debates about the advantages and disadvantages of alternative dietary regimes are likely to continue. The author of one pamphlet (The Socialist Party, 2000:17) writes that 'inter-supply of some foods would take place between the tropical and temperate regions'. That is an obvious, but by no means the only, way in which food and drink may be transported beyond the locality in which it is produced.

Work, not employment

All employment involves work, but not all work is employment. Even in capitalism, some work is done outside the employer-employee relationship: domestic work, voluntary work, some of the things done as leisure which are hard work but enjoyed by those who choose to do them. In socialism there won't be employees and employers, but there will be work. Many activities done in the course of employment are needed only to service capitalism — useless and destructive activities of many different kinds. The pamphlet quoted above gives the following, but the list is by no means exhaustive:

> Banking, insurance, finance and legal workers, chartered accountants, cost accountants, estimators, valuers, claims assessors, underwriters, brokers, taxation workers, marketing and sales personnel, advertisers, social security workers, cashiers and check-out assistants, police, prison workers, security guards, charities, armies, navies, air forces, armament workers, defence establishments, *etc*.

It is difficult to estimate the proportion of capitalist employment that won't be needed in socialism. Somewhere between 50 and 90 percent seems a fair guess. In any case, there will be a big increase in the numbers of people available for the production and distribution of useful goods and services directly for need. The increase can be turned to advantage in various ways. Working days, weeks, years and lifetimes could be shorter. Things now made cheaply (and often shoddily) to save labour time, and hence provide more profit for the employer, could be made by more labour-intensive methods, providing both a better product and more satisfaction to the worker. Morris foresees that there may be a shortage of work — perhaps, in some areas and for a brief time. But with people educated to use their imagination and not sitting around waiting to be told what to do, I can't see this being a serious problem.

Capitalism has elevated work to a very high position among the values which are thought to characterise a decent life and a good society. The idle rich are not held up as exemplars, and the idle poor suffer many deprivations. The heroes are not workers in the Marxian sense: they are people (some workers but mainly capitalists) who devote their whole lives to making money. Deferring to industry (production, measured by profit), other segments of society are subservient. Education (as we saw in chapter 9) is mostly about training for a job, not for life. Leisure is often looked on askance: it means forgetting about work as a means to an end and doing something as an end in itself. Capitalism is more comfortable with recreation than with leisure. Recreation is in the service of work — it is an industry in which you can find employment and an activity which is supposed to re-create you for the next bout of work.

The currently prevailing relationship between work and leisure — one largely of opposition or at least containment of the two spheres — will change markedly with socialism. Today only a fortunate few are able to make a living doing or making things that they would want to continue doing or making even if they had no need for money. Marx's 'free expression of each' is part of this process, as is Morris's perception that road-mending — and by extension many of the other activities that we tend to think of as onerous work — can become like enjoyable leisure.

Lateral organisation and communication

Within capitalism much research is devoted to finding the best way to organise production. Organisation is closely bound up with control, which we shall consider in detail in the next chapter. Here we shall focus on how production is organised in capitalism and likely to be in socialism, depending partly on what kind of activity is being organised and partly on the social context in which the organisation operates.

In capitalism organisations tend towards one of two main patterns: hierarchical or lateral (more simply tall, thin organisations or short, fat ones). Hierarchical organisations have a lot of management levels, one on top of the other. The extreme case is only one person at each level: A reports to B, B reports to C, *etc*. Lateral organisations have few levels of management, with many individuals at each level. The extreme case is only one level — no one manages or bosses anyone else.

A more complex way of looking at organisations is to divide them into mechanistic and organic types. Burns and Stalker (1994:119–122) go into considerable detail about this, but the following summary of the main points will suffice here.

Mechanistic organisations (and systems of management) are appropriate to stable conditions. Specific but fairly narrow rights and responsibilities are attached to each functional role; the structure of control, authority and communication is hierarchical; and interaction between members tends to be vertical and one-way (orders down from above, information up from below).

Organic systems are appropriate to changing conditions. There is a wider range of rights and responsibilities for each functional level; there is a network structure of control, authority and communication; and a lateral rather than a vertical direction of interaction and communication (sideways consultation rather than command from above).

In socialism there will be little scope for mechanistic organisations and systems of management. Instruction in the sense of 'this is the way to do it' will still be needed; instruction in the sense of 'do it because I say so' won't. However, at least in the early stages of socialism, it is possible that some people will prefer either to give or to take orders. Some will regard themselves (probably correctly) as being better than average organisers, while others will be quite happy to be organised, at least for some purposes. Also the routine work necessary only to capitalism, and which lends itself to mechanistic organisation and management, will disappear. With participation in organic forms of production and management, the gap between chiefs and Indians will narrow, if not disappear.

Another way of looking at organisations is to ask: who is their prime beneficiary? Blau and Scott (1963:42–58) discern four types. Again, we can summarise.

Mutual-benefit associations primarily benefit their own members. Examples destined to disappear with capitalism are political parties, war veterans' organisations and religious sects. Trade unions will not need to function to protect the interests of their members against those of employers, but may well join with professional associations to bring together people who share an interest in certain kinds of work.

Business concerns primarily benefit their owners. They will all disappear with socialism. The word 'business' has a dual meaning in capitalism. It stands for the organisations and activities of buying and selling, but also for procedures which may be used by non-business organisations, for example, items on an agenda may be referred to as 'business'. In that sense, there will no doubt continue to be 'socialist business'.

Service organisations have the basic function of serving clients. Included in this category are social work agencies, hospitals, schools and mental health clinics. Service organisations such as legal aid societies will not have a place in socialism. While most service organisations may be expected to continue in socialism, it is probable that, along with other measures to promote equality, the gap between 'professionals' and 'clients' will tend to narrow.

Commonweal organisations have the public at large as their prime beneficiary. Examples of commonweal organisations that won't be needed in socialism are those of military services, police and tax authorities. Other types that probably will find a place in socialism include fire services, environmental protection bodies (though they won't have to battle with short-term profit seeking businesses), and the research function in universities.

Clearly much more could be discussed about the ways in which organisation and communication in socialism will differ from the forms they take in capitalism. Cook (2000:219f) sees technology playing a big part in future communication: more and better computers, electronic democracy, internet newsgroups, and so on. I attach more importance to human, social developments than to technological, computerised ones. But it is a matter of 'both...and' not 'either...or'. There will surely be variations around the world in respect of types of organisation and communication, their specialisms and their relative frequency.

Increased long-term perspective

Capitalism is ambivalent about the short term and the long term. Capital accumulation itself is supposed to be the result of thrift, of saving part of what is earned to invest later. According to Cohen (1955), middle-class values (which may be equated with capitalist values) include 'an orientation to long-run goals and long-deferred rewards' (p.88) and 'a readiness and an ability to postpone and subordinate the temptation of immediate satisfactions and self-indulgence in the interest of the achievement of long-run goals' (p.89).

Yet capitalism is keen, and on occasions even desperate, to get people to 'buy now, pay later'. Few ideas are less musical to capitalist ears than 'save for a rainy day' (except, of course, those capitalists profiting from the savings industry). Deferred gratification is definitely not good for business. The dominance of the short-term perspective is seen in any number of ways: in causing irreparable damage to the environment by pursuing quick profit, by compelling poor people to plant 'cash' crops to pay interest on debts, by running down public services to save tax, by encouraging day trading on the stock exchange, and so on. Even the projects that will take decades to complete are often not what is most needed to improve the living conditions of people generally. We are supposed to get excited about putting men on Mars around 2015 — the same year in which some politicians promise to halve the number of the world's population living in poverty. On past form, Mars will win.

In socialism all three perspectives — short, medium and long — will be taken into account in planning and decision making as appropriate. At the outset, priority will probably have to be given to meeting basic needs. The author of the pamphlet quoted earlier (The Socialist Party, 2000:15) makes a reasonable prediction of the situation:

> Socialism must immediately stop people dying from hunger; it must ensure adequate food production. It must house the world's population in comfort, providing for the basic necessities of piped clean water, drainage systems, decent cooking facilities and so on. In socialism we must establish a safe world energy supply, stop pollution and adopt techniques which could work within the natural systems of the environment in non-destructive ways. We must bring into balance the world distribution of means of production and transport systems, storage facilities, *etc*. We must extend health services, education facilities, and further develop communications of every kind. For this work, socialism would begin with a structure of production which is distorted by waste and the arms race, and is inadequate for all the real needs of the community.

I have no quarrel with this statement, except the implication of the last sentence. The structure of production that socialism will begin with will be a structure at the very end of capitalism's life as a world system. That system may still be distorted by waste and the arms race. But who knows how it may have been forced to change as a result of pressure from the growing socialist movement?

Chapter 17

DEMOCRATIC CONTROL

Capitalism	*Socialism*
Authoritarian and some limited democratic control of social processes	Democratic control of social processes
Emphasis on competition Periodic elections to choose professional politicians	Emphasis on co-operation Elections as required to choose delegates or representatives
Leaders and followers	Participants, not leaders and led

Having dealt in previous chapters with ownership and production, we now focus on control. Arguably the most important form of control in any society is that which is designed to maintain it as a system. In capitalism the emphasis is on competition, although co-operation is necessary for some purposes. In socialism the emphasis is on co-operation, although benign forms of competition look set to continue. Then we consider questions concerned with elections: capitalist professional politicians and the extent to which delegates or representatives may be appropriate in socialism. Finally we discuss leadership and followership — endemic in capitalism but questionable in socialism.

Democratic control

It is not essential to capitalism that governments are elected to power. With a passive majority, power may simply be seized by a determined group backed by armed force. However, history shows that some form of democracy — even if only token — helps to run the system more effectively than dictatorships. Even dictators who refuse to accept the possibility of being overthrown are usually, if reluctantly, prepared to submit themselves to the popular vote, especially if they can rig it in their favour.

The advantage to the ruling class in having a majority vote in favour of the system that privileges them is that 'the people' are put on their side instead of being the enemy. As Perrin (2000:28) observes, 'the parliamentary system has generally emerged as the most effective way of ensuring the domination of the capitalist class in society, making laws and providing for their enforcement'. Although authoritarian governments still persist (notably in the less economically developed parts of the world), Perrin is right to speak of 'the present era of collapsed dictatorships'(p.29). There is no reason to suppose that supporters of capitalism will wish to abandon the rhetoric, and some of the substance, of democracy. As long as all candidates at elections stand for unchanged or reformed capitalism, the world is safe for bourgeois democracy.

Socialists today share with supporters of capitalism a positive view of the principle of democracy. In the past some socialists were sceptical about the parliamentary road to socialism. Unfortunately, disdain for parliament and electoral activity laid the basis for vanguardism — a movement of self-appointed 'socialist' leaders (and non-socialist followers) who would capture political power on behalf of the workers. But the achievement of socialism depends on a majority of socialists understanding what the new society means and organising to achieve it. With the state machine controlled by elected anti-socialist and non-socialist representatives, any attempt to take power by meeting the might of the armed forces head on would be disastrous.

Socialist literature contains frequent references to the 'capture' of political power and the 'establishment' of socialism. There is some justification for this usage. It is not conceivable that socialism can be introduced without having a democratic majority take over the powers of government in order that they 'may be converted from an instrument of oppression into the agent of emancipation' (Declaration of Principles, The Socialist Party). But 'establishment' carries the meaning of something done fairly quickly, like establishing a business on a particular day. In fact this interpretation is supported by another socialist saying (now increasingly regarded as a joke): 'Speed the day'. None of us knows how long it will take for control of the world system to pass from 50+ percent of the population supporting capitalism to 50+ percent supporting socialism. But the process will certainly take much longer than a day.

Emphasis on co-operation

In the capitalist economy competition is more apparent than co-operation. Business enterprises compete with one another for sales of commodities, and workers are forced to compete with one another for jobs. Nation states, each acting on behalf of their own 'economies' (business interests), compete with other nation states in a win-lose situation. Trade wars sometimes lead to 'hot' wars. However, capitalism also requires some measure of co-operation to function effectively. To maximise profits capitalist enterprises seek to control the 'free market' in their own favour. They get together to agree not to undercut each other's prices to consumers, not to give workers more than minimum wage concessions, and sometimes to restrict output to keep up prices.

Capitalists like to have workers competing with each other for jobs. They encourage this by preferring to give them individual, short-term contracts rather than 'jobs for life'. A reserve army of unemployed labour is good for keeping employed workers on their toes, fearful of losing the jobs that have kindly been 'created' for them by their employers. Most employers do their best to discourage workers from joining trade unions. They are quite willing to withdraw their capital from enterprises that don't promise profit, but they use their control of the media to harden public opinion against workers who withdraw their labour (go on strike).

With socialism there will be a much different relationship between competition and co-operation, What may be called benign forms of competition will no doubt continue — I gave the example of non-professional competitive sport in chapter 15. Capitalism in other areas of life may well be valued and enjoyed, although more by some individuals than others. Who is the most ...? who has produced the best ...? who has done most to ...? are questions that will interest at least some people. Will there be world champions of this, that or the other? My answer is probably yes. I rather like the idea of Marx being voted thinker of the second millennium.

Socialism will put much more emphasis on co-operation than capitalism does. The building of a socialist world will require the co-operative efforts of virtually everyone (a few 'obstinate refusers' can be tolerated). It is therefore important not to underestimate the extent of change that will be needed in people's attitudes to each other and to society. In capitalism there is no great need to foster co-operation, certainly not at the world level (activities like international flight control and weather forecasting are the exception rather than the rule). The idea of doing something for the 'community' without reward is now not unknown, but usually takes second place to doing something for oneself or one's family.

People are said to be at their best, at their most pro-social, when faced with disasters, such as wars, floods or fires. Socialism will entail pro-social behaviour as a matter of course, not as exceptional. There will be plenty of opportunities to show what Kohn (1990) calls the brighter side of human nature. Co-operation means sharing in planning and decision making, not having plans and decisions imposed on oneself or imposing them on others. Such co-operation can exist happily with benign forms of competition.

Representatives or delegates?

According to most dictionaries, there isn't much difference between a representative and a delegate. Representatives are chosen or elected to positions in which they are supposed to act on behalf of others. Delegates are chosen or elected to act for or represent others. The small difference, however, can be crucial. Representatives are not bound to carry out the decisions or wishes of those who appoint them. Delegates are.

In capitalist democracies representatives are elected to parliament (or to a house of representatives) for either a fixed period or until such time as the government decides to call another election. These representatives are almost always professional politicians — they have an income from being elected, even though that may not be their main source of income. Once elected, they may represent their constituents in only the loosest sense of that term. Nearly all of them are members of a political party, and there is pressure on them to support party policy, irrespective of their own views. There is, however, little or no pressure on them to carry out the wishes of their constituents, except insofar as they may judge that supporting or opposing certain policies may help to get re-elected.

The principle of generally having delegates rather than representatives is consistent with how socialist society will be controlled. It is a more democratic form of control than is typical in capitalism, but it need not (and in my view should not) exclude representation.

Delegates are mandated by their constituents to carry out policies arrived at as a result of democratic discussion and subsequent majority decision. They are subject to recall if they don't abide by majority decisions. Their constituents may not wish to mandate delegates on some issues. Also, with some controversial issues it may be thought desirable to hear the views of other delegates before coming to a decision. In both cases, delegates are given a 'free hand' and act more like representatives.

One view of socialist democratic decision making is that it will involve three main levels:

> A democratic system of decision-making would require that the basic unit of social organisation would be the local community which could elect delegates to a local council which could be given the responsibility for local administration... Then, regional councils could provide organisations through which decisions affecting wider populations could be made at the regional level. Similarly, global decisions could be made by delegates elected to a world council (The Socialist Party, 2000:8).

In principle the idea of having levels of decision making something like the above is sensible. But it may turn out that socialist levels won't bear much resemblance to current local, regional and global levels. I'm not saying that we shouldn't now discuss such matters of detail. I am saying that, as the socialist movement grows, we mustn't imagine that capitalist structures and arrangements will remain more or less unchanged. We must be prepared for some surprises.

Participants, not leaders and led

The question of what to do about leadership is an important one for socialists. We know that capitalism relies on having leaders and followers. We know that socialism cannot be achieved by a knowledgeable vanguard leading an ignorant mass. But in what sense, if any, will socialism need leaders? Let me set the scene for discussion with this somewhat ancient but almost lyrical quotation:

> ... populous and powerful societies, in all the designs of living thus far developed among humans, are governed by a favoured few who rule over unprivileged or less privileged multitudes. The few may be priests or nobles, militarists or merchants, plutocrats or commissars, managers or mandarins. The many may consist of slaves or serfs, burghers or wage-earners, citizen-commoners or collective farmers. 'Rule' may mean cruel exploitation, inspired leadership or benevolent protection. Yet the pattern of power is everywhere the same, regardless of whether the elite is hereditary, appointive or elective, or whether the prevailing ideology is Confucianism, Capitalism, Communism, or what not. Every elite is unsafe. Every mass is prone to envy

> and hatred of superiors. To deflect the resentments of the multitudes away from those who rule them and against foreign foes and domestic pariahs has ever been the most efficacious means of maintaining the loyalty of masses toward elites, preserving the social order against subversion or revolution, and reinforcing the bonds of shared emotion without which no community can function (Schuman, 1952:106).

Schuman makes some good points and it's difficult to deny that that's the way things have mostly been. But he's no socialist. Nowhere in his book does he even hint that what has happened in the past may not have to happen in the future. He is not alone in his views. There is a substantial literature on leadership, but most of it assumes, or clearly states, that it is here to stay. Gardner (1984:325) is typical: 'We can have the kinds of leaders we want, but we cannot choose to do without them.'

It seems to be generally agreed that leadership involves a relationship between leaders and led. Leadership is not something possessed by the leaders but rather a relationship in which the followers and their characteristics are as important as the leaders and their characteristics (Barnes, 1967:67). This is confirmed by the training given to potential leaders recruited into the West Point Academy: 'We begin by teaching them to be followers' (Litzinger and Schaefer, 1984:138).

A socialist approach to leadership is well expressed by Nair (1994:139): 'We are all leaders. Each one of us is setting an example for someone else, and each one of us has a responsibility to shape the future as we wish it to be.' In capitalism followers far outnumber leaders, with this result: we are (nearly) all followers. Each one of us has an example set for us by someone else, and each one of us lets others take responsibility for shaping the future.

In capitalism leadership, regarded as an ability possessed by some people but not others, is often treated as portable from one area of life to another. Thus a 'celebrity' in one field, such as sport, is expected to live up to celebrity status in another field, such as entertainment. In socialism it is likely that more attention will be paid to developing everyone's potential than to elevating some to celebrity status. If someone paints a number of acclaimed pictures, gives excellent theatrical performances, makes an outstanding contribution to a particular branch of science, their achievements will no doubt be recognised — but they won't be worshipped as demi-gods.

Apart from the question of what part, if any, leadership has to play in future socialist society, there is the more urgent matter of leadership in the socialist movement today. Perrin (2000:194f) selects leadership as one of the four main problems facing the Socialist Party, the others being its over-legalistic conception of revolutionary change, its cumbersome internal democracy, and why its propaganda has not resulted in more members. Perrin points out that over nearly a hundred years of existence the Socialist Party of Great Britain (its formal title) has not developed a leadership. He believes that the emergence of a leadership, 'though not impossible, is an unlikely prospect... because the members will not let it.' Opposition to political leadership is one of the basic requirements of SPGB membership.

Perrin believes that the SPGB's policy of no leadership may result in finding 'its currently developing relationship with the media a difficult one...' I shall have more to say about the developing socialist movement in the last chapter, but the question of socialists and the capitalist media can be dealt with here. We must aim to develop, as soon as possible, a socialist network of media information and communication, not to rely on the capitalist media to publish or broadcast only what they wish about us. We have started on this road by taking advantage of the relatively free internet by creating our own websites, engaging in electronic debates, *etc*. We must publish more hard copy, make more tapes and videos, advertise their availability more widely. These and other further developments will need money, and lots of it. We must move towards controlling the discussion of socialist ideas ourselves and away from having them controlled by the capitalist media.

Chapter 18

FREE ACCESS

Capitalism	*Socialism*
Access by economic demand (mostly payment, some handouts)	Free access, each determining their own needs in social context
Markets (buying, selling and exchange) for most things including labour	No buying, selling or exchange, only giving and taking
Calculation in money	Calculation in kind
Education for élites and masses	Education for all

The last of the four interdependent themes of socialism may be summed up as free access — the 'to each according to his needs' Marxist maxim. First we examine the consequences of changing from a social system which generally denies access to goods and services except by economic demand (money) to one in which access is based directly on need (no money). We then look at markets — for buying, selling and exchange in capitalism and (if the word shopping continues to be used) for picking up or enjoying the things that are needed. Capitalist calculation in terms of money will give way to socialist calculation in kind. Finally, there is the key issue of education, which must play an essential part not only in changing society from unfree to free access but also in all the other ways in which it will help to realise the human potential to move from capitalism to socialism.

Free access

We may see mode of access as the fourth leg on which any society stands. In capitalism ownership of property means that labour is employed by capital to produce things only when there is prospect of profit, the system is controlled in the interest of the minority of capitalists, and access to what is owned, produced and controlled is primarily by economic demand (money). In socialism there is common ownership (no ownership), things are produced because people need them, the system is controlled in the interest of everyone, and access to what is commonly owned, produced and controlled is free within reasonable limits.

Having expressed my view that free access is the fourth leg of socialism, I must acknowledge that for other socialists the system has only three legs. Perrin (2000:169) writes of socialism as 'based on common ownership of the means of production and distribution, democratic control, and production solely for use', although he does refer to people 'exercising their right of free access to consumer goods and services according to their self-defined needs, constrained only by what could be made available' (p.182). In another pamphlet (The Socialist Party, 2000:5) free access is linked with production for use, by which is meant 'bringing production into direct line with human needs... individuals will have free access to what is produced according to self-defined needs'.

It is not important that for some socialists the question of free access seems slightly less basic than the 'big three' of common ownership, democratic control and production for use. However, I would argue that production for use is meaningless without 'use' being defined as having access to what is needed. How far this access can be really 'free' is something we need to discuss, if only because some objectors to socialism claim it would never work because people's needs would always exceed society's capacity to meet them.

All socialists agree that in the new society people won't be told what they need — hence the common qualification 'self-defined' or 'self-expressed' needs. The further qualification 'constrained only by what could be made available' is a fairly loose constraint. There should be no problem with meeting basic needs and most of what might be called everyday needs, but catering for 'luxuries' could be another matter — perhaps resolved differently in various parts of the world. Cook (2000:157) gives the example of ornate or complicated garments and suggests that they will be available 'if someone is prepared to manufacture them, or they make them themselves'.

Giving and taking

A good way of summing up many of the differences between capitalism and socialism is to say that in the one the most common transaction is buying and selling while in the other it is giving and taking. As we saw in chapter 16, some work in capitalism is done outside the buying and selling of the wage-labour-capital nexus. There is giving and taking in families and sometimes between friends or neighbours; also state and private charity. Exchange is a typically capitalist relationship because it implies private ownership of that which is exchanged. Buying and selling can both be regarded as forms of exchange — money is given in exchange for the thing bought and received in exchange for the thing sold.

So deeply entrenched is the use of money in all forms of property society — and especially in capitalism — that it is not easy to contemplate a world without it. Most economists regard money as having three main functions: as a medium of exchange, a unit of account and a store of value (Lipsey and Chrystal, 1995:673). Sometimes other functions are added, such as being a standard of deferred payments, or even 'a vehicle used to create, experience and maintain social and family relationships and establish distinctions between moral and immoral, masculine and feminine, self and community' (Thompson, 2000:170).

In explaining how necessary and useful money is, economists always compare it favourably with barter, never with free access. They recognise that there are such things as free goods (and services) but 'economic man' prefers to sideline them. Indeed, capitalism, the predator, looks on free goods as prey, to be brought to the market for commercial consumption if at all possible.

The opposite of free access is unfree access, or paid-for access. Rifkin (2000) has recently written a book with a most revealing subtitle, 'The new culture of hypercapitalism where all of life is a paid-for experience'. His main thesis is that 'ownership is steadily being replaced by access' (p.4) and that 'sellers and buyers are replaced by suppliers and users, and virtually everything is accessed' (p.6). Rifkin believes that:

> We are making a long-term shift from industrial production to cultural production... Global travel and tourism, theme cities and parks, destination entertainment centers, wellness, fashion and cuisine, professional sports and games, gambling, music, film, television, the virtual worlds of cyberspace and electronically mediated entertainment of every kind are fast becoming the center of a new hypercapitalism that trades in access to cultural experiences (p.7).

He overstates his case. Ownership hasn't been replaced by access, and people are still buyers and sellers. It is undeniable that capitalism today trades much more than it did in the past on cultural experiences, but it still trades in such basics as food, clothing and shelter. Rifkin's analysis is focused on the First World and ignores the Third World. Nothing in what he and other writers have had to say on 'hypercapitalism' can lead us to suppose that developments within capitalism are somehow leading us towards a world of free access. He makes this clear in his comments on the electronic superhighway:

> The coming together of computers, telecommunications, cable television, consumer electronics, broadcasting, publishing and entertainment in an integrated communications web allows commercial enterprises to exercise unprecedented control over the ways human beings communicate with one another (p.219).

If giving and taking — as opposed to buying and selling — are to grow within capitalism then it won't be as a result of developments in information and communications technology. It will be because more and more people will come to see that nonmonetary relationships which normally work very well within families and some households can be extended to society as a whole — but only if society's members wish to make those socialist relationships work.

Calculation in kind

This brings us to the question of the use of money as a means of calculating the most efficient methods of production, and how socialist society could operate without monetary calculation but only with calculation in kind. Perrin (2000:175f) devotes 14 pages to discussion of this matter. My brief summary below is intended as an introduction to, not a substitute for, those pages. I also want to add a few words on whether socialists have sufficiently thought through the implication of calculation in kind in the growing sphere of cultural production.

It is alleged by critics of socialism that without money and markets it would be impossible to calculate whether one good was 'worth' more than another in terms of costs incurred in producing it. Owing to its inability to reduce all the factors of production to a common denominator (money), socialism — it is claimed — would have no mechanism for deciding the most efficient use of resources, or even whether a given product should be made at all. Instead of calculation of economic value, socialism would have to rely on vague estimates to guide its plans. Two solutions to this problem have been proposed: labour time accounting (labour vouchers, as considered by Marx for the early stages of socialism) or millions of simultaneous equations. Neither solution has appealed to the supporters of free access.

The challenge to find a workable alternative to economic calculation has been taken up by the advocates of 'natural' calculation or calculation in kind:

> ... it is perfectly possible to calculate 'costs' without resorting to prices and this is done all the time today: how much energy does this process consume per unit of output compared with another; which strain of wheat yields greater output; does this product use up more of a particular resource spread over the lifetime of the product than a comparable product; is the productivity of workers sorting mail by hand more or less than in the case of automatic sorting, taking into account the labour embodied in the machinery used? (Perrin, p.180).

Though calculations and choices will still have to be made, there would be no need to employ a common unit of cost accounting such as money. Instead we would need to have a system of self-regulating stock control, based on the type of operation already used by retail outlets in capitalism. Need would be expressed as required quantities of materials and goods which would be communicated to production units. The process would be self-regulating because production would be adjusted to the communication of material requirements. If stock built up, production would be reduced; if it became low, production would be increased.

The proposals regarding stock control have so far assumed that 'production' is concerned only with materials and goods. Further thought needs to be given to how free access can be applied to cultural production. Although some items of cultural production may well disappear with capitalism — for example, gambling (except perhaps as a game, not a financial transaction) — I see no reason to doubt that other items will continue. On a world scale they may even increase, as basic needs are met and other needs come to the fore. Calculation in terms of kilos, litres or cubic metres will need to be supplemented by calculation in terms of visits made, seats occupied, courses attended and experiences accessed. Not all of these calculations will lend themselves to stock control. I'm not saying that free access to items of cultural production will present an insoluble problem to socialism. I am saying that something other than stock control — maybe first come, first served, waiting lists, ballots, even short-term rationing — may be appropriate responses.

Education for all

Education is crucial in determining whether we live in a capitalist world or a socialist one. We have capitalism today because young people are taught its norms and values, its customs and its institutions, and older people by and large continue to accept what they have come to regard as normal.

Education in capitalism is designed to reproduce the next generation in the same mould as existing adult generations. As we saw in chapter 9, there is elite education for the rich and mass education — essentially training for a job — for the majority. Young people are taught that you can get things only if you pay for them; begging and stealing are frowned-upon options. If you work hard you can own things. You don't have to work hard if you have rich parents, win a big jackpot, or can 'succeed' in business (find a way of exploiting the work of others). Your motive to produce is profit if you are an employer, or a wage or salary if you are an employee. And control of the kind of society you live in is something you exercise every few years when you elect a government to 'power'.

There is education required to bring about socialism, and education as a feature of socialist society. First, education to help build socialism. Every new generation of socialists needs to be educated to replace those who make up their final time sheet. But by recruiting people into the Socialist Party rather than into the socialist movement we run the risk of over-playing the political, and under-playing the educational, role in promoting revolutionary change. While the capture of political power is an important element in the building of socialism, such power is impotent unless it is exercised by a majority who are educated to understand and want such a fundamental change in society.

At present the effort put into education to help build socialism is severely limited by the very small number of active socialists and by lack of money. In Britain there is a monthly journal the *Socialist Standard* which is addressed both to socialists, for whom it mostly provides material for educating themselves and others, and to potential socialists, for whom it is a source of learning about socialism. Every encouragement is given to members and sympathisers to engage in socialist propaganda (a word we are not all comfortable with because of its fascist connotation). This is done by attending meetings, talking, writing, sending e-mails, getting on talk-back shows, *etc.*

But, with so few people taking part in these essentially educational activities, the smooth surface of capitalism's dominance of ideas is scarcely scratched.

Now imagine what could happen if many more people were to become active socialists and much more money were to be spent on the socialist educational project. A weekly journal and then a daily newspaper, much more advertising about socialism and socialist publications in the capitalist media, theatre performances of plays such as Howard Zinn's *Marx in Soho*, films and/or videos of Morris's *News from Nowhere*. Schools, colleges, universities and distance learning projects could be set up which treated capitalism critically and socialism sympathetically, instead of the other way round. Such educational developments, to be fully effective, would need to be linked with mutually reinforcing developments in publishing, electronic communication, the arts, leisure and small communities of like-minded people.

Socialists at least as far back as Morris have speculated on how education in general, and of children in particular, will differ in socialism as compared with capitalism. Morris wrote dismissively (and in what would now be regarded as sexist terms) of schools in capitalism as 'boy farms'. Regarding education in *Nowhere*, he sought to narrow the difference between learning manual skills and book-learning. His own sympathies seem to lie more with the former ('we don't encourage early bookishness').

Cook (2000) follows Morris's general line on education in socialism, although with a much greater technological input: 'Children as well as older people will be able to use [libraries, museums and art galleries] to explore and investigate the information, ideas and controversies that interest them... places where, as well as books and exhibits, the bulk of the world's knowledge will gradually be built up on computer databases...' (p.175). I accept that Morris's pre-electronic age predictions need updating, but as somewhat of a technophobe I would wish education in socialism not to be so dominated by electronic gadgetry as current education is in the First World and as it threatens to be in the Third World.

Chapter 19

A FUTURE FOR SOCIALISM

This final chapter is by way of a conclusion to the whole book. My main theme throughout has been that, while capitalism is now immensely strong and in some ways is still in process of conquering the world, it will not last for ever as a dominant world system. I assume that what will take its place will be something that it is sensible to call socialism (or communism, or whatever: its name is not important, its substance is). The first thing to realise is that the revolution, when it comes, will be a comprehensive one, a fundamental change in the whole of society, not just a change in one or more of its parts. We must accept that the revolution we are seeking is a process, not an event — we are in it for the long haul. A few socialists have outlined different scenarios; no doubt many others will be proposed as time goes on. Finally, why is it a good idea to stop supporting capitalism and to start today to build a socialist world of the future?

The comprehensive revolution

Revolution has three common meanings, two of which are misleading as regards socialism. Revolution is sometimes seen as meaning violent, as opposed to peaceful, means of achieving social change. As an adjective it can be used to inflate a small change to make it appear bigger, a synonym for 'new', as with a revolutionary new washing powder. Neither of those meanings is relevant to socialism, which means a fundamentally different form of society from capitalism.

The socialist revolution will be comprehensive because it will have consequences for every part of the social fabric. This doesn't mean that all changes will be of equal extent and importance. Traditionally, socialists have insisted on the primacy of the political role — the capture of political power has been seen as the key event. But the majority of socialists who will participate in that event won't just be political animals — they will also be economic, educational, cultural, social and many other kinds of animal. Any manifestation of human life and society that has been coloured by capitalism will now have a socialist hue.

According to Burbach and his colleagues (1997:155), 'it will not just be the proletariat, but a much larger group of economic actors involved in an array of achievements at the grassroots who will slowly shape a new alternative and carry out the new social revolution'. Obviously for those authors the 'proletariat' describes only a minority of the population. There is also a worry that 'grassroots' — always a vague term but generally describing those in subordinate positions — will exclude the future equivalents of people like Marx, Engels and Morris. But the general point of Burbach et al is valid: the socialist revolution will be the work of many people in many social situations, and cannot be the work of a few only in a restricted part of the whole system.

When talking about the whole of society we have to realise that 19th century capitalism was a much less complex form of society, with roots less deep in working-class consciousness, than is 21st century capitalism. In his review of five centuries of capitalism, Beaud (1983:228) notes the change in mentality needed from 'them and us' to 'different kinds of us':

> It is not that the advance toward socialism is impossible, but that it is more complex than the great visionaries of the 19th century ever imagined; it involves not only the socialization of the means of production but also the liberation from the millenia-long habits of dependence and submission.

Comprehensive revolution does not necessarily mean that there is no continuity between the past and the present, and that therefore we must expect no continuity between late capitalism and early socialism. Certain changes can be made at a given hour on a given day — a new organisation formally set up, a new set of rules relating to conduct of a certain kind. But the socialist revolution, in all its complexity, cannot be by 'one fell swoop'. As Lewis (1972:262) observes, 'The transition from capitalism to socialism will be a long, intricate and confused affair involving the whole thought pattern or world view now prevailing'.

In for the long haul

First the bad news. The short-term prospects for socialism could hardly be more gloomy. Let three voices, one British , one American and one Australian, say something about the full extent of the prevailing capitalist hegemony:

Few things seem more remote today than socialism... The abandonment of any socialist goals by parties still bearing the name has only added more confusion and futility for many more who once thought socialism a goal worth fighting for... over a hundred years ago the appeal of socialism was simple: it was the rule of the working class. The 20th century has dealt ruthlessly with this original vision of socialism as democratic working-class rule... no existing social system competes with capitalism for the future... the system itself operates more nearly in its pure and simple market-driven form than it has for most of the 20th century... with few exceptions the state and the institutions of capitalist politics have been captured by neoliberal/ conservative movements and politicians... Across the world the traditional mass parties of the working class and the political left are more conservative than ever — more removed from the ideas of socialism and from their working-class base... The organizations of the revolutionary socialist left, which might more rightfully lay claim to the kinds of political ideas that embody full-fledged socialist consciousness, are smaller and more fragmented than ever... the alternatives currently put forth by progressives and social democrats of all kinds, stakeholder capitalism, civil society/Third Sector counter force, *etc.*, do not offer much material solace to the world's majority. This majority cries out for something with more meat on its bones, something that capitalism has been increasingly less willing or able to deliver on a world scale for some time (Moody, 1997:293–308).

The great achievement of the ruling establishment in the last 30 years or so has been to use every opportunity, notably the collapse of the Soviet Union, to persuade people that we are prisoners of a system from which there is simply no escape...the establishment has managed to convince many people that there is nothing beyond the capitalist horizon and, therefore, that you can do no more than tinker with the system... Despite the depth of popular discontent and anxiety today, the number of people convinced that their own vital problems can be solved by reshaping society is very limited. Indeed, it is smaller than it was, say, 30 years ago... we must ponder why people now have less confidence in the possibility of moving beyond the reign of capital than their ancestors did more than 150 years ago... the old order is a-dying, in so far as it can no longer provide answers corresponding to the social needs of our point of development, though it clings successfully to power because there is no class, no social force ready to push it off the historical stage (Singer, 1999:152–4, 258–79).

> ... the colossus of capitalism, against which socialism reacted and was first formed, now stands unchallenged astride the global system... yet everywhere we are in chains, ranging from the actual servitude of low pay and daily violence to the symbolic chains of two-party politics and 'choice' between McDonald's and Hungry Jacks or Burger King (Beilharz, 1994:54).

The socialist movement, never strong, is now in bad shape. Impostors have got it a bad name, the working class has let it down, the few genuine socialists lack resources and are poorly organised, 'There Is No Alternative' rules, tinkering with the system appears all that can be done. Capitalism is failing to meet people's needs, but it still clings to power.

To overcome all these obstacles will take time — most probably a lot of time. That does not mean that nothing can be done until we judge 'the time is ripe'. We can start the process today, though the goals we set ourselves may not be achieved in our lifetime (when I use the analogy of the medieval craftsman working on a cathedral that won't be finished in his lifetime, most of my comrades don't like it, so I won't repeat it here). We can start to build socialism now — or, more precisely, those of us who have not yet participated in the socialist movement can resolve to do so. The act of withdrawing support from capitalism is the first step. It leads logically to the next step: taking part with other socialists in the construction of the new society.

What is involved in withdrawing support from capitalism? One thing you can do is to refuse to vote for any electoral candidate who supports capitalism. You have to be very careful about this. Few candidates make a point of declaring 'I support capitalism', but you can be sure that most of them do. Since they are united in not wanting revolutionary change, they urge you to vote — preferably for them, next best for one of their capitalism-supporting opponents, worst of all for none of them. Because there are so few socialists, it is rare that you will have a socialist candidate to vote for. But you can still show your rejection of capitalism by writing 'Socialism' across your ballot paper.

Something can be done on the individual level besides voting. If you reject capitalism it is a good idea to try to get others to do the same. You can talk to people about it, either individually or in groups, write letters, articles or books, send e-mails, try to get on talk-back shows, *etc*. You can also set an example by your own personal conduct. Because of your rejection of the money system you may be urged to give all your money away. Assuming that you have some to give away, this is not a helpful suggestion, unless the beneficiary is something connected with the socialist movement.

It is usually a good idea to practise what you preach. But it's doubtful how far this actually helps the progress of socialism. Would it have made any differences to Marx's immense contribution to socialist ideas if he had not married a titled lady and not had an occasional punt on the stock exchange? My own view is that, provided we don't harm others in the process, we should take every opportunity of getting as much out of capitalism as we can — and then being generous in our donations to the socialist movement. Capitalism doesn't even feel the pinpricks resulting from a few poor workers pooling their pennies to fight it. But an educational campaign financed by a socialist Bill Gates or Warren Buffett may well see the movement take off.

I don't want to downplay what can be done on the level of personal conduct because, as part of the development of socialist education, I can see the need for the setting up of small and then larger socialist communities. Utopian attempts to opt out of property-based society to set up more or less self-sufficient communities have a poor record of survival. But such attempts have usually failed because their members were not sufficiently detached from capitalist values.

Korten (1998), in a book subtitled 'life after capitalism', suggests that we should 'consider taking a lower-paying job doing work that has real meaning with a values-led, community-based organization or enterprise that is contributing to the life of the community and the planet' (p.268). A few people are doing that sort of thing already, and more will no doubt do so in the future. Such action does not necessarily make them socialists, and their example could be taken as showing that capitalism recognises, and even praises, their behaviour. Ritzer (1993), an opponent of McDonaldisation, thinks that, instead of being a customer, you should do as many things as you can for yourself — including, of course, passing up lunch at McDonald's. It's hardly a revolutionary gesture, but maybe it's better than nothing.

Alternative scenarios

When people outline scenarios of the future they are rarely indifferent to what they predict. They either want it to happen or not to happen. They either want it to be a self-fulfilling prophecy or to be a warning of dire consequences if avoiding action is not taken. There are capitalist scenarios and socialist scenarios. First a taste of the capitalist ones. Berry (1995) looks ahead to the next 500 years:

> There will in general be two classes of workers: those who earn their living by giving orders to machines, and those who go deep into space in search of precious asteroids. But they will have no cause for mutual antipathy. like capitalists and labourers in the last two centuries. For the labourers will themselves be capitalists! The enterprise of mining the asteroids will be entirely private. The people who do it will be in individual companies in competition with one another (p.248).

Not a very exciting prospect — unless mining asteroids turns you on! Dertouzos (1997) looks ahead only two centuries, but comes up with a Work-Free Society:

> The people of the world will do no work, because they will derive all the revenue they need to buy their desired goods and services from the machines that they own. Machines will make the machines that are needed too... Everyone will be a capitalist because all people will own machines and other income-producing capital assets... with all that leisure time on their hands, people are likely to help others on a grand scale — which would make them good socialists' (p.274).

You can either treat that 'scenario' as a joke or take it seriously. If it isn't a joke then it's a nightmare — a world of machine-owning workless people who help others only in their leisure. Bronowski (1978:18) surely had something better than that in mind when he wrote that 'human consciousness depends on the ability to imagine'.

Now for the socialist scenarios. As the quote from Leonard at the beginning of this book suggests, it is not a good idea to try to paint a detailed picture of the future (except as an example, as Morris did). Those who have done so in the past, particularly if they have attempted to predict future mechanical inventions and social habits extrapolated from the present, have often come unstuck. For instance, in 1975 it was predicted that by 2000 small recreational submarines would be common, the average age of retirement would be 50, and 'weekends' would be distributed throughout the week (Veal, 1987:135). But that shouldn't put us off outlining the main ways in which future socialism will differ from present capitalism. 'The people at the time will decide' is a sensible approach to take to details. But a more pro-active stance is needed for the principles.

In chapters 15–18 I have suggested that socialism will be a society featuring common ownership, production solely for use, democratic control and free access. I have sought to show that, just as the main features of capitalism (private ownership, production for profit, authoritarian or limited democratic control and access by economic demand) constitute a whole system, so socialism will have parts that mesh with each other and with the whole.

Any socialist scenario should be clear enough to unite people in its energetic pursuit, but not so detailed as to divide them in its planned practice. Today's socialists tend to give priority either to demolishing capitalism or to building socialism. The common ground on which they meet is that the demolition of capitalism is in order to build something better and the construction of socialism is a response to the problems and inadequacies of capitalism.

A rough indication of which of these two streams of socialist thought you favour is whether Marx or Morris played the more significant part in making you a socialist. If forced to come off the fence, I land on the Morris side. But the fence ought to be as low as possible. Marx and Morris reinforce, rather than oppose, each other.

Singer (1999:261) makes a suggestion that I find provocative: people 'may rebel, explode, and break out in anger, but quite understandably they will not join a long-term movement of social transformation... unless they know where it is heading and how it is proposed to get there.' How far is this true? Unquestionably there is a lot of rebellion, explosive feeling and anger, but not much of it knows where it is heading and how to get there. A case in point is the much-publicised anti-capitalist movement and its campaigns of protest and disruption in various cities against multinational corporations. In terms of changing society fundamentally, it's achieving very little, if anything positive at all. I risk being divisive in saying so, but the anti-capitalist movement is not a socialist movement — at best it is preparatory to it and at worst a distraction from it.

Building socialism

The most devastating critique of capitalism as a system achieves nothing positive if it doesn't lead on to action to replace it by a fundamentally different and better form of society. The intellectual marriage of Marx and Morris has produced a small family of 20th century socialists who are struggling to multiply in the new century. At least the idea of socialism is alive, cruelly distorted by capitalism-preserving impostors though it has been. And we can all surely agree with Beilharz (1992:129) that, after all the travails since the Enlightenment, through the Age of Revolutions to the epoch of holocausts, humanity deserves a better prospect than the utopia of the hamburger.

There are three outstanding questions I want to conclude by tackling. First, can we reasonably claim that today socialism is a practical alternative? Second, assuming that we know what we are (intellectually) fighting for, who or what is our enemy? And third, does capitalism have a future, though not as a dominant world society?

Over the last two decades there has been an initiative within the Socialist Party to work out among ourselves, and then present to others for wider discussion, proposals to support the claim that socialism is a practical alternative to capitalism. These efforts have resulted in working papers, a pamphlet, and several articles in the *Socialist Standard*. While I strongly agree that we must be as positive as we can about socialism, I can see some dangers in presenting it as 'practical' in the sense of matter-of-fact or easy to achieve. The biggest danger is that, if we base our plans on a 'socialist' take-over of existing capitalist institutions and agencies, we give the impression that socialism is just capitalism without money.

I referred in chapter 17 to the authoritarian and libertarian strands of thought within the socialist movement. I mean something very similar to what Crump (1995) calls the 'social democratic' and the 'anarchist' view of socialism. The social democratic view of socialism sees the institutions and agencies of capitalism being taken over and 'socialised' and 'democratised', changing their functions from servicing capital to serving society. The anarchist view is that the institutions and agencies of capitalism must be dismantled and transcended, assuming that bodies which are useful for capitalist purposes cannot be adapted for socialist ones. Crump believes that socialism will involve a synthesis of these two views: it will blend new institutions and agencies with those that are taken over from capitalism and transformed. I agree with him, but have other concerns about the two views.

The social democratic approach is too much of a piecemeal, politics-led one, and not enough of a comprehensive, politics-inclusive one. The Socialist Party pamphlet (2000:6) states '... socialists organised in their local areas would probably prepare programmes of action for immediate implementation once the movement has gained control of the powers and machinery of governments.' In a small concession to comprehensiveness, it is also stated that 'the practical ways in which [democratic administration and production solely for needs] will begin, as part of various community actions to deal with problems, will have been prepared in advance of the capture of political control' (p.7).

This isn't good enough. It implies that the capture of political power will be the signal for plans to become actions. But a moment's imaginative thought will show that a complex, functioning society cannot wait upon the political whistle before it starts the new game. None of us can know this far in advance how the details of the synchronised change will work out, but we'll be advancing on all fronts, not just the political one.

The anarchist approach has to be careful not to react too strongly against 'politics' and not to underplay the importance of building new structures to replace capitalist ones. I don't mind the Houses of Parliament being adapted for more sweet-smelling uses, but I do question whether bodies on a 'mote' scale will be adequate to cope with democratic control on a world socialist scale. Perhaps I'm too much of a creature of capitalism, but I do prefer people and groups and organisations to be efficient as well as pro-socialism. And I do like the trains to run on time, whether capitalist or socialist.

My second question is: who or what is our enemy? I don't think anyone or any group should be cast as our enemy. Neither individual capitalists nor the capitalist class as a whole is our enemy — it is the capitalist system we oppose. According to Blackwell and Seabrook (1988:115), 'Whereas the socialist myth relies upon the growing consciousness of one class, the green myth depends upon the self-realization of all humanity.' They are using myth in the sense of a collective belief built up in response to the wishes of a group. My point is that the humanity they claim for the green myth should be an attribute of the socialist myth. The basic division is — Socialists are people who understand, want and work for socialism. Anti-socialists oppose socialism and non-socialists make it impossible (which comes to the same thing).

The question of class affiliation concerns capitalism and is not crucial to beliefs about socialism. Whether you are a worker (in the vast majority) or a capitalist (in a tiny minority), you may be either in the socialist group (presently tiny) or the other group (anti- plus non-socialists, presently the overwhelming majority). Only if you believe that socialism is essentially about dispossessing the capitalists and giving the workers more possessions will you insist that the class struggle is the same as the struggle for socialism. It isn't.

Let me put this another and perhaps slightly softer way. Because workers are the overwhelming majority in capitalist society, they will be the overwhelming majority who will replace that system with socialism. The capitalist class is not an enemy to be defeated — the ideas supporting capitalism (held by both workers and capitalists) are an obstacle to be overcome. I'm sorry if this treads on traditionally working-class toes, but ex-capitalists are as entitled as ex-workers to participate in the socialist world society.

Lastly, the controversial question of whether capitalism has a long-term future. I hope it doesn't shock you too much to learn that I think it does. A system that has held sway for at least five centuries will surely not be swept into oblivion. In socialism I believe that many people will still be fascinated by the idea and the practice of capitalism. Games like monopoly will be based on simulated capitalist relationships, the rise and fall of capitalism will be taught alongside the rise and fall of the Roman Empire, museums will feature capitalist artefacts and memorabilia, re-enactments of events and campaigns in capitalist times will be educational as well as entertaining diversions, although not to everyone's taste.

It is generally agreed among today's socialists that the new society will be a tremendously varied, developmental and stimulating one. The arrangements for common ownership, production for use, democratic control and free access will lend themselves to a wide variety of interpretations. Many socialists believe there will be resistance to the new socialist arrangements from members of the capitalist class who will be 'dispossessed'. Coming from such a tiny numerical minority, such resistance could only be a problem for the socialist majority if it were supported by a sizeable number of workers, who would presumably see themselves as being dispossessed of the right to live in capitalism.

It seems to me reasonable to suppose that some people will take more easily to socialism than others. For most of the population a life in socialism will be fine. But for some it may be a problem. The 'problem' group may turn out to be two groups: those who love to be leaders and those who are content to be followers. The two groups complement each other, need each other. It may be that the leaders will be people with exceptional talent of some kind, though I don't think the 'best brains' will generally be averse to contributing to a socialist world. The followers may be one brain cell short of an Einstein

— or they may simply want to poodle along in life without the responsibilities of a normal socialist citizen.

*

The most difficult task facing those who want to build socialism today is to get others to join them. Reforms are tempting short-term fixes and can be implemented quickly. The whole weight of the capitalist hegemony is behind the status quo or reforms of it. Yet revolution, though its perspective is long term, is also a sensible short-term policy. Once capitalism is seriously challenged by those who insist that it must be replaced and show at least in outline how this can be done, it can only respond by offering concessions in the direction of socialism. Capitalism will never be the same again — and the socialist revolution will have begun.

Bibliography

Agnew, J. and Corbridge, S., *Mastering Space: Hegemony, Territory and Political Economy*, London, Routledge, 1995.

Albert, M., *Capitalism Against Capitalism*, London, Whurr, 1995.

Applebaum, H., *The Concept of Work: Ancient, Medieval and Modern*, Albany, N.Y., State University of New York Press, 1992.

Avineri, S., *The Social and Political Thought of Karl Marx*, London, Cambridge University Press, 1971.

Bahro, R., *Socialism and Survival*, London, Heretic Books, 1982

Bang, J., 'Ideological sources of communes in Britain', in Y. Gorni *et al*, eds., *Communal Life*, New Brunswick, NJ, Transaction Books, 1987.

Barber, B., *Jihad versus the World*, New York, Random House, 1995.

Barnes, S.H., 'Leadership styles and political competence', in L. J. Edinger, ed. *Political Leadership in Industrialized Societies*, New York, Wiley, 1967.

Beaud, M., *A History of Capitalism 1500–1980*, New York, Monthly Review Press, 1983.

Beder, S., *Global Spin: the Corporate Assault on Environmentalism*, Melbourne, Scribe Publications, revised edn. 2000.

Beilharz, P., *Labour's Utopia: Bolshevism, Fabianism, Social Democracy*, London, Routledge, 1992.

——, *Postmodern Socialism*, Melbourne, Melbourne University Press, 1994.

Berry, A., *The Next 500 Years: Life in the Coming Millennium*, London, Headline, 1995.

Biel, R., *The New Imperialism: Crisis and Contradictions in North-South Relations*, London, Zed Books, 2000.

Blackwell, T. and Seabrook, J., *The Politics of Hope*, London, Faber, 1988.

Blau, P.M. and Scott, W.R., *Formal Organizations: A Comparative Approach*, London, Routledge, 1963.

Bonefeld, W. and Holloway, J., *Global Capital, National State and the Politics of Money*, London, Macmillan, 1995.

Bocock, R., *Hegemony*, Chichester, Ellis, Horwood, 1986.

Bookchin, M., *The Modern Crisis*, Philadelphia, PA, New Society Publishers, 1986.

——, *Remaking Society: Pathways to a Green Future*, Boston, South End Press, 1990,

Bowles, S. and Gintis, H., *Democracy and Capitalism*, New York, Basic Books, 1986.

Brenner, Y. S., *Capitalism, Competition and Economic Crisis*, Brighton, Sussex, Wheatsheaf Press, 1984.

Bronowski, J., *The Origins of Knowledge and Imagination*, New Haven, Yale University Press, 1978.

Brown, L., Renner, M. and Halweil, B., *Vital Signs 1990/2000: the Environmental Trends That Are Shaping Our Future*, London, Earthscan, 1999.

Bryan, L. and Farrell, D., *Market Unbound: Unleashing Global Capitalism*, New York, Wiley, 1996.

Buick, A., 'Ollman's vision of communism', *Critique*, 9, Spring–Summer, 1978.

——, and Crump, J., *State Capitalism: the Wages System under New Management*, New York, St, Martin's Press, 1986.

Burbach, M., Nunez, D. and Kagarlitsky, B., *Globalization and its Discontents*, London, Pluto, 1997.

Burgmann, V., *In Our Time: Socialism and the Rights of Labour 1885–1905*, Sydney, Allen & Unwin, 1985.

——, *Power and Protest: Movements for Change in Australian Society*, St. Leonards, NSW, Allen & Unwin, 1993.

Burkett, P., *Marx and Nature: A Red and Green Perspective*, New York, St. Martin's Press, 1999.

Burns, T. and Stalker, G., *The Management of Innovation*, 3rd edn., Oxford, Oxford University Press, 1994.

Butsch, R., *For Fun and Profit*, Philadelphia, Temple University Press, 1990.

Callon, M., *The Law of the Markets*, Oxford, Blackwell, 1998.

Carnoy, M., 'Multinationals in a changing world economy', in M. Carnoy *et al.* eds. *The New Global Economy in the Information Age*, University Park, Penn State University Press, 1993.

Carter, A., *Marx: a Radical Critique*, Brighton, Sussex, Wheatsheaf, 1988.

Catley, B., *Globalising Australian Capitalism*, Cambridge, Cambridge University Press, 1996.

Chomsky, N., 'Propaganda and control of the public mind', in R.

McChesney *et al*, eds., *Capitalism and the Information Age*, New York, Monthly Review Press, 1998.
Coates, D., *Models of Capitalism*, Cambridge, Polity, 2000.
Cohen, A. K., *Delinquent Boys*, New York, Free Press, 1955.
Cohen, P., 'Teaching enterprise culture', in I. Taylor, ed., *The Social Effects of Free Market Policies*, Hemel Hempstead, Harvester-Wheatsheaf, 1990.
Coleman, S., *Stilled Tongues*, London, Porcupine, 1997.
——, ed., *Reform and Revolution: Three Early Socialists on the Way Ahead*, Bristol, Thoemmes, 1996.
——, and P. O'Sullivan, eds. *William Morris and News from Nowhere*, Bideford, Devon, Green, 1990.
Cook, R., *Yes, Utopia! We Have the Technology*, Birmingham, Cook, 2000.
Cotgrove, S., *Catastrophe or Cornucopia: Environment, Politics and the Future*, Chichester, Wiley, 1982.
Coveney, P. and Highfield, R., *Frontiers of Complexity: the Search for Order in a Chaotic World*, New York, Ballantine Books, 1995.
Craig, N. *Alternative World*, London, Housmans Bookshop Publishers, 1997.
Crosland, C. A. R., *The Future of Socialism*, London, Cape, 1956.
Crump, J., 'Changing things'. Paper to Socialist Party Weekend Conference, Sept. 1995.
Cullen, S., *The Last Capitalist*, Freedom Press, 1996.
Daly, H. and Cobb, J., *For the Common Good: Redirecting the Economy Toward Community, the Environment and a Sustainable Future*, Boston, Bincor Press, 1989.
Dawson, M. and Foster, J., 'Virtual capitalism', R.M. Chesney *et al.*, eds, *Capitalism And the Information Age*, New York, Monthly Review Press, 1998.
Dertouzos, M. L., *What Will Be: How the New World of Information Will Change Our Lives*, New York,.Harper Collins, 1997.
Dugger, W. M.,'Class and evolution', in R. Bauman *et al.*, eds., *Political Economy and Contemporary Capitalism*, New York, Armonk, 2000.
Dymski., G. and Elliott, J., 'Capitalism and the democratic economy;' in E. Paul *et al*, eds., *Capitalism*, Oxford, Blackwell, 1989.
Edgar, A. E., 'Oscar Wilde and socialism', *Socialist Standard*. Nov. 2000.
Elgin, D. and Mitchell, R., 'Voluntary simplicity', *The Futurist*, October, 1977.

Engels, F., *Anti-Duhring*, London, Lawrence and Wishart, 1936.
Etzioni, A., *The Spirit of Community*, London, Fontana, 1995.
Fetscher, I., 'Marx, Engels and the future society', *Survey*, Oct. 1961.
Flett, K. and Renton, D., eds., *The 20th Century: A Century of Wars and Revolutions*, London, Rivers Oram Press, 2000.
Follett, M. P., *Freedom and Co-ordination*, London, Management Publications Trust, 1949.
Frank, R. and Cook, P., *The Winner-Take-All Society*, London, Penguin, 1996.
Frank, T., *One Market Under God*, London, Secker and Warburg, 2001.
Froissart, J., *Chronicles*, Harmondsworth, Middx., Penguin, 1968.
Fukuyama, F., *The End of History and the Last Man*, London, Hamish Hamilton,1992.
Galbraith, J. K., *The Culture of Contentment*, London, Penguin, 1993.
Gardner, H., *Leading Minds: an Anatomy of Leadership*, London, Harper Collins, 1984.
Gates, J., *The Ownership Solution: Towards a Shared Capitalism for the 21st Century*, London, Allen Lane, 1998.
Ghebre, M., 'Education under capitalism', *Socialist Standard*, July, 1994.
Gianaris, N. V., *Modern Capitalism: Privatization, Employee Ownership and Industrial Democracy*, Westport, CT, Praeger, 1996.
Gibson-Graham, J. K., *The End of Capitalism (as we know it)*, Oxford, Blackwell, 1996.
Giddens, A., *The Third Way and its Critics*, Cambridge, Polity, 2000.
Girling, J., *Capital and Power: Political Economy and Social Transformation*, London, Croom Helm, 1987.
Gorz, A., 'Work and consumption', in P. Anderson and R. Blackburn, eds., *Towards Socialism*, Ithaca, Cornell University Press, 1966.
Goudie, A., *The Human Impact on the Natural Environment*, Cambridge, Mass., MIT Press, 5th edn. 2000.
Gray, J., *False Dawn: the Decline of Global Capitalism*, London, Granta Books, 1998.
Green, F. and Sutcliffe, B., *The Profit System: the Economics of Capitalism*, Harmondsworth, Middx., Penguin, 1987.
Green, J., *Taking History to Heart: the Power of the Past in Building Social Movements*, Amherst, University of Massachusetts Press, 2000.

Greider, W., *One World, Ready or Not: the Manic Logic of Global Capitalism*, New York, Simon & Schuster, 1997.

Halal, W., *The New Management: Democracies and Enterprise Are Transforming Organizations*, San Francisco, Berrett-Kohler, 1996.

Handy, C., *The Hungry Spirit: Beyond Capitalism*, New York, Broadway Books, 1998.

Harvey, D., *The Limits to Capital*, Chicago, Chicago University Press, 1982.

Haseler, S., *The Super Rich: the Unjust New World of Global Capitalism*, London, Macmillan, 2000.

Haywood, T., *Information Rich, Information Poor: Access and Exchange in the Global Information Society*, London, Bowker-Saur, 1995.

Hetner, R. W., *Market Cultures*, Oxford, Westview Press, 1998

Heilbroner, R., *Twenty-first Century Capitalism*, Concord, Ontario, Ananci, 1992.

——, *Visions of the Future: the Distant Past, Yesterday, Today and Tomorrow*, Oxford, Oxford University Press,1995.

Hiebert, R. and Gibbons, S., *Exploring Mass Media for a Changing World*, Mahwah, NJ, Lawrence Erlbaum Associates, 2000.

Hill, S., 'Britain: the dominant ideology thesis after a decade', in N. Abercrombie *et al.*, eds. *Dominant Ideologies*, London, Unwin Hyman, 1990.

Hirst, P., *Associative Democracy: New Forms of Economic and Social Governance*, Amherst, University of Massachusetts Press, 1994.

Hodgson, A., *The Romances of William Morris*, Cambridge, Cambridge University Press, 1987.

Hodgson, G., *Capitalism, Value and Exploitation*, Oxford, Martin Robertson, 1982.

Hollander, P., *Soviet and American Society: a Comparison*, New York, Oxford University Press, 1973.

Holloway, J., 'Capital is class struggle', in W. Bonefeld and J. Holloway, eds., *Post-Fordism and Social Formation*, London, Macmillan, 1991.

Hutton, W., *The State to Come*, London, Vintage, 1997.

—— and Giddens, A., eds., *On the Edge: Living with Global Capitalism*, London, Vintage, 2001.

Hyde, L., *The Gift: Imagination and the Erotic Life of Property*, London, Vintage.

Jay, G., *Lather and Whitewash*, Socialist Standard, September, 1986.

Jenkins, D., *Market Whys and Human Wherefores*, London, Cassell, 2000.

Jenkins, P., *Mrs Thatcher's Revolution: the Ending of the Socialist Era*, Cambridge, Mass., Harvard University Press, 1988.

Kagarlitsky, B., *The Twilight of Globalization*, London, Pluto, 2000.

Keane, J., *The Media and Democracy*, Cambridge, Polity, 1991.

Kelly, K., *New Rules for the New Economy*, London, Fourth Estate, 1998.

Klein, N. *No Logo, No Space, No Choice, No Jobs*, Toronto, Knopf, 2000.

Kohn, A., *No Contest: the Case Against Competition*, Boston, Houghton Mifflin, 1986.

——, *The Brighter Side of Human Nature*, New York, Basic Books, 1990.

Kolakowski, L., *Re-structuring the World Economy*, New York, Pantheon Books, 1978.

Kolko, J., *Restructuring the World Economy*, New York, Pantheon Books, 1988.

Korten, D. C., *When Corporations Rule the World*, London, Earthscan, 1995.

——, *The Post-Corporate World: Life After Capitalism*, San Francisco, Berrett-Kohler, 1998.

Kropotkin, P., *Mutual Aid: a Factor of Evolution*, London, Allen Lane, 1972.

Laclau, E. and Mouffe, C., *Hegemony and Social Strategy*, London, Verso, 1985.

Lam, M. C., 'A resistance role for Marxism: in the belly of the beast', in S. Makdisi *et al.*, eds., *Marxism beyond Marxism*, London, Routledge, 1996.

Lane, D., *Politics and Society in the USSR*, London, Weidenfeld and Nicolson, 1970.

Lane, R. E., *The Market Experience*, Cambridge, Cambridge University Press, 1991.

Lawson, N., 'Some reflections on morality and capitalism' in E. Paul *et al.*, eds., *Capitalism*, Oxford, Blackwell, 1989.

Lean, G., 'The giving age has been postponed', *New Statesman*, 18 Dec. 1998.

Le Guin, U., *The Dispossessed*, New York, Avon, 1974.

Leiman, M., 'Introduction to Karl Marx and Friedrich Engels' in R. Romano and M. Leiman, eds., *Views on Capitalism*, Beverly Hills, CA, Glencoe Press, 1970.

Leonard, G. B., *Education and Ecstasy*, London, Murray, 1970.

Levinson, D. and Christensen, K., *The Global Village Companion*, Santa Barbara, CA, ABC-CLIO, 1996.

Lewis, J., *The Marxism of Marx*, London, Lawrence and Wishart, 1972.

Lipsey, R. and Chrystal, K., *An Introduction to Positive Economics*, Oxford, Oxford University Press, 8th edn. 1995.

Liston, D. P., *Capitalist Schools: Explanation and Ethics in Radical Studies of Schooling*, London, Routledge, 1988.

Litzinger, W. and Schaeffer, T., 'Leadership through followership', in W. Rosenbach and R. Taylor, eds., *Contemporary Issues in Leadership*, Boulder, CO, Westview Press, 1984.

Lomborg, B., *The Sceptical Environmentalist*, Cambridge, Cambridge University Press, 2001.

London, J., *The Iron Heel*, London, Newnes, n.d.

McCaughey, D., *Tradition and Dissent*, Melbourne, Melbourne University Press, 1997.

McLellan, D., *The Thought of Karl Marx*, London, Macmillan, 1971.

McQueen, M., *The Essence of Capitalism*, Sydney, Hodder Headline, 2001.

Mandela, N., 'The waning nation state', in N.P. Gardels, ed., *At Century's End: Great Minds Reflect on Our Time*, La Jolla, CA, ALTI Publishing, 1996.

Marquand, D. C., *The New Reckoning: Capitalism, States and Citizens*, Cambridge, Polity, 1997.

Martin, H. and Schumann, H., *The Global Trap: Globalization and the Assault on Prosperity and Democracy*, London, Zed Books, 1997.

Marx, K., *A Contribution to the Critique of Political Economy*, International Library Publishing Co., 1904.

——, *Capital*, Moscow, Progress Publishers, 3 vols. 1954-9.

——, *Critique of the Gotha Programme*, New York, International Publishers, 1977.

——, and Engels, F., *The German Ideology*, New York, International Publishers, 1845.

——, *The Communist Manifesto*, London, 1848.

——, *Selected Works*, Moscow, Foreign Languages Publishing House, 1935.

Mattelart, A., *Multinational Corporations and the Control of Culture*, Brighton, Sussex, Harvester, 1979.

Meadows, D. H. *et al.*, *Beyond Limits: Confronting Global Collapse, Envisioning a Sustainable Future*, Post Mills, VE, Chelsea Green Publishing 1992.

Meier, P., *William Morris: the Marxist Dreamer*, 2 vols. 1978.

Mies, M. and Bennholdt-Thomsen, V., *The Subsistence Perspective, Beyond the Globalised Economy*, London, Zed Books, 1999.

Miliband, R., *Socialism for a Sceptical Age*, Oxford, Polity, 1994.

Mills, C. W., *The Power Elite*, New York, Oxford University Press, 1956.

Monbiot, G., *Captive State: the Corporate Takeover of Britain*, London, Macmillan, 2000.

Moody, K., *An Injury to All: the Decline of American Unionism*, London, Verso, 1988.

——, *Workers in a Lean World*, London, Verso, 1997.

Moore, S., *Marx Versus Markets*, University Park, Penn State University Press, 1993.

Morris, W., *News from Nowhere*, London, Penguin, 1984.

Morrison, J., *Reforming Britain: New Labour, New Constitution?*, London, Pearson Education, 2001.

Morris-Suzuki, T., 'Capitalism in the computer age', in J. Davis *et al*, eds., *Cutting Edge: Technology, Information Capitalism and Social Revolution*, London, Verso, 1997.

Morton, A. L., *The English Utopia*, London, Lawrence & Wishart, 1952.

Mosbacher, M. *Marketing the Revolution*, London, Social Affairs Unit, 2002.

Nair, K., *A Higher Standard of Leadership: Lessons from the Life of Gandhi*, San Francisco, Berrett-Koehler, 1994.

New Statesman, 'Having his way and eating it', editorial, 25 Sept. 1998.

Nielsen, K., 'Socialism and egalitarian justice', in J.P. Sterba, ed., *Social and Political Philosophy: Contemporary Perspectives*, London, Routledge, 2001.

Northcott, J., *Britain in 2010*, London, Policy Studies Institute, 1991.

Novak, M., *The Spirit of Democratic Capitalism*, New York, Simon & Schuster, 1982.

Nove, A., *The Economics of Feasible Socialism*, London, Allen & Unwin, 1998.

Offe, C., *Contradictions of the Welfare State*, London, Hutchinson, 1984.

Ollman, B., 'Marx's vision of communism: a reconstruction', *Critique*, 8, Summer, 1977.
Paczuska, A., *Socialism for Beginners*, London, Writers & Readers Publishing Co-operative, 1986.
Peet, R., *Global Capitalism: Theories of Societal Development*, London, Routledge, 1991.
Pepper, D., *Eco-Socialism, From Deep Ecology to Social Justice*, London, Routledge, 1993.
Perrin, D., *The Socialist Party of Great Britain: Politics, Economics and Britain's Oldest Socialist Party*, Wrexham, Bridge Books, 2000.
Pierson, C., *Socialism After Communism*, University Park, Penn State University, 1995.
Pilger, J., *Hidden Agendas*, London, Vintage, 1998.
——, *Distant Voices*, London, Vintage, 1994.
Plant, S. E., *The Joy of Capitalism*, Harlow, Longman, 1985.
Porritt, J., *Seeing Green*, Oxford, Blackwell, 1984.
Redwood, J., *The Global Marketplace: Capitalism and Its Future*, London, Harper Collins, 1993.
Reich, K. B., *The Work of Nations: Preparing Ourselves for 21st Century Capitalism*, New York, 1991.
Rheingold, H., *Virtual Reality*, New York, Simon & Schuster, 1991.
Rifkin, J., *The Age of Access: the New Culture of Hypercapitalism Where All of Life Is a Paid-for Experience*, New York, Penguin Putnam, 2000.
Ritzer, G. *The McDonaldization of Society*, Newbury Park, CA, Pine Forge Press, 1993.
Robinson, J., *The Manipulators: The Conspiracy to Make Us Buy*, London, Simon and Schuster, 1998.
Rodley, G., 'Promoting the sporting ethos', in S. Rees and G. Rodley, eds., *The Human Costs of Managerialism*, London, Pluto, 1995.
Rueschemeyer, D. and Evans, P., 'The state and economic transformation', in P. Evans *et al*, eds., *Bringing the State Back In*, London, Cambridge University Press, 1985.
Sahlins, M., *Stone Age Economics*, Chicago, Aldine, 1972.
Sale, K., *Rebels Against the Future*, Reading, Mass., Addison-Wesley, 1995.
Sampson, A., *The Midas Touch*, London, Hodder & Stoughton, 1989.
Sanderson, S. K., *Social Transformations: A General Theory of Historical*

Development, Oxford, Blackwell, 1995.

Schor, J., *The Overworked American*, New York, Basic Books, 1991.

Schuman, F. L., *The Commonwealth of Man*, New York, Knopf, 1952.

Schweikart, D., *Against Capitalism, Cambridge*, Cambridge University Press, 1993.

Scott, J., *Corporate Business and Capitalist Classes*, Oxford, Oxford University Press, 1997.

Seabrook, J., *The Everlasting Feast*, London, Allen Lane, 1974.

Seldon, A., *Capitalism*, Oxford, Blackwell, 1990.

Shaw, B., *The Intelligent Woman's Guide to Socialism, Capitalism, Sovietism and Fascism*, Harmondsworth, Penguin, 1971.

Sherman, H. J., 'A Marxist view of class and evolution', in R. Bauman *et al*, eds., *Political Economy and Contemporary Capitalism*, New York, Armonk, 2000.

Shutt, H., *The Trouble With Capitalism: An Enquiry Into the Causes of Global Economic Failure*, London, Zed Books, 1999.

Silk, L. and Silk, M., *Making Capitalism Work*, New York, 20th Century Fund, 1996.

Singer, D., *Whose Millennium? Theirs or Ours?*, New York, Monthly Review Press, 1999.

Singer, M. and Wildavsky, A., *The Real World Order*, New Jersey, Chatham House, 1993.

Singer, P., *Marx*, Oxford, Oxford University Press, 1980.

Singman, J. L., *Daily Life in Medieval Europe*, London, Greenwood Press, 1999.

Slaughter, S. and Leslie, L., *Academic Capitalism*, Baltimore, The John Hopkins University Press, 1997.

Smith, A., *The Wealth of Nations*, Oxford, Clarendon Press, 1986.

Smith, K., *Free Is Cheaper*, Gloucester. John Ball Press, 1988.

——, *The Survival of the Weakest*, Gloucester, John Ball Press, 1994.

Snooks, G. D., *The Dynamic Society: Exploring the Sources of Global Change*, London, Routledge, 1996.

The Socialist Party of Great Britain, Ecology and Socialism, London, 1990.

——, *Socialism as a Practical Alternative*, London, 2000.

Soros, G., 'The capitalist threat', *Atlantic Monthly*, Feb.1997.

——, *The Crisis of Global Capitalism*, London, Little, Brown,1998.

Sowell, T., *Marxism: Philosophy and Economics*, New York, Morrow, 1985.
Standage, T., *The Victorian Internet*, London, Weidenfeld & Nicolson, 1998.
Staples, W. G., *The Culture of Surveillance*, New York, St. Martin's Press, 1997.
Stratman, D., *We Can Change the World*, Boston, New Democracy Books, n.d.
Suter, K., *Global Agenda: Economies, the Environment and the Nation State*, Oxford, Lion Publishing, 1995.
Talbott, S. L., *The Future Does Not Compute: Transcending the Machines in Our Midst*, Sebastopol, CA, O'Reilly & Associates, 1995.
Taylor, A., *Choosing Our Future: A Practical Politics of the Environment*, London, Routledge, 1992.
Teeple, G., *Globalization and the Decline of Social Reform*, Toronto, Garamond Press, 1995.
Thomas, G., 'Marx's basic theory', *Socialist Standard*, Feb. 1998.
Thompson, E. P., *William Morris: Romantic to Revolutionary*, London, Merlin Press, 1977.
Thompson, N., 'Social opulence, private asceticism; ideas of consumption in early socialist thought', in M. Daunton and M. Hilton, eds., *The Politics of Consumption*, Oxford, Berg, 2001.
Thompson, V. E., *The Virtuous Marketplace*, Baltimore, The John Hopkins Press, 2000.
Titmus, R., *The Gift Relationship: from Human Blood to Social Policy*, London, Allen & Unwin, 1971.
Tomlinson, A., ed. *Consumption, Identity and Style*, London, Routledge, 1990.
Trainer, T., *Towards a Sustainable Economy: the Need for Fundamental Change*, Oxford, Carpenter, 1996.
Tressell, R., *The Ragged Trousered Philanthropists*, London, Lawrence & Wishart, 1956.
Turner, B. S., 'Commercialization, peroration on ideology, in N. Abercrombie *et al.*, eds., *Sovereign Individuals of Capitalism*, London, Allen & Unwin, 1986.
Veal, A. J., *Leisure and the Future*, London, Allen & Unwin, 1987.
Venable, V., *Human Nature: the Marxian View*, New York, Knopf, 945.
Wachtel, P., *The Poverty of Affluence*, London, Collier Macmillan, 1983.

Walker, A., *Marx: His Theory and Its Context*, London, Longman, 1978.
——, 'The strategy of inequality', in I. Taylor, ed., *The Social Effects of Free Market Policies*, Hemel Hempstead, Harvester Wheatsheaf, 1990.
Wallace, I., *The Global Economic System*, London, Unwin Hyman, 1990.
Walzer, M., *Spheres of Justice: A Defence of Pluralism and Equality*. New York, Basic Books, 1983.
Weiss, L., *The Myth of the Powerless State*, London, Polity, 1998.
White, G., *Revolutionary Socialist Development in the Third World*, Brighton, Sussex, Wheatsheaf, 1983.
Wilde, O., *The Soul of Man Under Socialism*, London, Humphries, 1912.
Wood, E. M., *Democracy Against Capitalism*, Cambridge, Cambridge University Press, 1995.
——, 'Labor, class and state in global capitalism', in E. M. Wood *et al.*, eds., *Rising from the Ashes? Labor in the Age of Global Capitalism*, New York, Monthly Review Press, 1998.
Worster, D., 'The vulnerable earth', in D. Worster, ed., *The Ends of the Earth: Perspectives on Modern Environmental History*, Cambridge University Press, 1988.
Wright, A., Socialisms: *Theories and Practices*, Oxford, Oxford University Press, 1986.
Zinn, H., *Marx in Soho*, South End Press, 1999.

Index

access, free *vii–viii, xii*, 14, 108–9, 142–7
advertising 45, 66, 71, 80, 82
Agnew, J. 37
Albert, M. 62
alienation 26, 28
anarchism, *xi*, 95, 127, 156–7
Applebaum, H. 18
armed forces *xi*, 17, 135
Avineri, S. 99

Bahro, R. 120
Bakunin 102
Ball, John *xi*
Bang, J. 92
Barber, B. 39
Barnes, S. H. 140
Beaud, M. 150
Beder, S. 80
Beilharz, P. 105, 152, 156
Bennholdt–Thomsen, V. 96
Berry, A. 163
Biel, R. 116
Blackwell, T. 157
Blair, Tony 42
Blau, P. M. 132
Bocock, R. 82
Bolshevism, 29, 59
Bonefeld, W. 55
Bookchin, M. 86
bourgeoisie 28, 80, 91, 101
Bowles, S. 41
Brenner, Y. S. 40, 114
Bronowski, J. 154
Brown, L. 46
Bryan, L. 67
Buick, A. 53, 100
Buffett, W. 153
Burbach, M. 59
Burgmann, V. 55, 87
Burkett, P. 87
Burns, T. 131
Butsch, R. 78

calculation in kind xii, 145–6
Callon, M. 31
capital 24–5, 31, 33, 40, 56, 69, 75, 114, 142, 151, 156
capitalism *vii–xii*, 21–89, 92–4, 97, 99, 105, 117–9, 124, 128–33, 142–50. 153, 155–9
Carnoy, M. 69
Carter, A. 105
Catley, B. 66
Charter 88 40, 93
Chartism 92
Christensen, K. 18
Chomsky, N. 77
class *viii, x*, 14, 16–7, 25, 78, 123–4, 157
  capitalist *ix*, 25, 50
  struggle *ix*, 24–5, 49–50, 157
  working *ix, xi*, 24, 28, 32, 40–1, 50, 54, 59, 63, 74, 98. 150–2
Coates, D. 62
Cobb, J. 97
Cohen, A. K. 133
Cohen, P. 73
Coleman, S. 75, 110, 115
commercialisation *ix*, 44, 56
commodities *x*, 18, 24, 46, 63, 71, 85
communism *vii*, 57, 59, 99–101, 104, 149
  primitive *viii*, 14–15
Communist Party 59
communitarianism *ix*, 41–2
competition *ix, xii*, 32, 36, 51
consumerism *ix*, 24, 42, 44–5, 82
consumption *viii, x*, 16–17, 24, 28, 32, 72, 79–82, 104, 117
control, democratic *vii, xii*, 135–41
Cook, P. 39, 47
Cook, R. 133 143, 148
co–operation *x, xii*, 14, 82, 137–8

Corbridge, S. 37
Cotgrove, S. 87
Coveney, P. 71
Craig, N. 54
crime xi, 107, 126
Crosland, C. A. R. 97
Crump, J. 53, 156

Daly, H. 97
Dawson, M. 56, 119
debt bondage 18–19
decision–making *viii, xii*, 42–3
democracy ix, 39–41, 49, 54, 59, 135–41, 151, 157 (see also social democracy)
  industrial 40
Dertouzos, M. L. 154
dialectic 23. 102, 127
Dugger, W. M. 50
Dymski, G. 40

Edgar, A. 94
education *x, xii*, 49, 61, 63, 68, 72–4, 77, 82, 101, 103, 110, 115, 117, 147–9, 153
efficiency ix, 33, 37, 57, 157
Elgin, D. 156
Elliott, J. 40
Engels, F. viii, 21–5, 27–8, 87, 93, 99, 150e
environment 13, 15, 58, 83–8
Etzioni, A. 42
Evans, P. 62
exchange *vii–viii*, 30–1
experiences *viii, x*, 47, 49, 65, 70–1, 76, 78, 144, 146
exploitation 24, 28, 31, 55, 74–5, 79, 91

family 16, 19, 60, 98, 144–5
Farrell, B. 67
fetishism of commodities 26
Fetscher, I. 102
feudalism *vii–viii*, 19–20, 35, 90
First World ix, 70, 148
Fleet, K. 46
Flemish weavers *viii*, 20, 48
Follett, M. P. 42
Foster, J. 56, 119
Fourier 22, 92
Frank, A. 39, 47
Frank, T. 46
Froissart 91

Galbraith, J. K. 78
Gardner, H. 140
Gates, J. 41, 153
Ghebre, M. 73
Gianaris, N. V. 37
Gibbons, S. 70
Gibson–Graham, J. K. 25
Giddens, A. 41–2
Gintis, H. 41
Girling, J. 39
globalisation *x*, 28, 42, 65–9
Gorz, A. 79
Goudie, A. 84
Gray, J. 69, 85
Green, F. 61, 110
green (movement) *x*, 83–8, 157
Green, J. 114
Greider, W. 50, 55–6, 84, 118

Halal, W. 97
Handy, C. 44
Harvey, D. 72
Haseler, S. 29
Haywood, T. 46
Hefner, R. W. 45
Hegel, F. 22
hegemony *x*, 60, 72, 78–80, 93, 115, 117, 150, 159
Heilbroner, R. 38, 45, 60, 117
Hiebert, R. 70
Highfield, R. 71
Hill, S. 79
Hirst, P. 92
Hodgson, G. 63
Hodgson, P. 107, 109
Hollander, P. 60
Holloway, J. 50, 55
human nature 45, 51, 77, 82
Hutton, W. 37. 41
Hyde, L. 37

inequality 37–8, 46–7
internet 46, 67

Jay, G. 76
Jay, P. 68

Jenkins, D. 38
Jenkins, P. 33

Kagarlitsky, B. 68
Keane, J. 76
Kelly, K. 66
Keynes, J. M. 63
Klein, N. 46
Kohn, A. 51, 95
Kolakowsky, L. 68
Kolko, J. 56
Korten, D. C. 86, 153
Kropotkin, P. 95

labour *viii*, 15, 17–20, 23–5, 31, 36–7, 48–9, 51, 56, 63–4, 69, 73–4, 104–5, 119
  division of 15, 33. 101
  theory of value 24
Labour Party *vii,* 29, 49, 92–3, 97, 103, 115, 117–8
Laclau, E. 49
Lam, M. C. 115
Lane, D. 59
Lane, R. E. 37
Lawson, N. 32
leaders(hip) *viii*, 76–7, 139–41, 158
Lean, G. 47
LeGuin, U. *xi*, 94
Leiman, M. 24
leisure 15, 50, 78, 80–1, 130–1, 154
Leninism 29, 59
Leonard, G. B. 154
Leslie, L. 74
Levinson, D. 18
Lewis, J. 150
Lipsey, R. 150
Liston, D. P. 73
Lomborg, B. 84
London, Jack *xi*, 94
Luddites, 92
Luxemburg, R. 119

McCaughey, D. 95
McDonald's 41, 66, 152–3
McLellan, D. 23
McQueen, M. 45
Mandela, N. 66
market(s) *vii, ix*, 30–2, 42, 45, 48–9, 53, 57, 62, 68, 105, 151
Marquand, D. C. 57
Martin, H. 47, 76
Marx, K. *viii, xi*, 20–9, 49–50, 54, 78–9, 87–8, 93–4, 97, 99–106, 109, 124–5, 130, 146, 150, 155
Mattelart, A. 81
Meadows, D. H. 84
media (mass) *x, xii*, 70, 73–8, 117, 141
Meier, P. 109
Mies, M. 96
Miliband, R. 79
Mills, Wright 62
Mitchell, R. 96
Monbiot, G. 73
money *xii*, 54–5, 69, 81, 119, 143, 145, 152, 156
Moody, K. 114, 151
Moore, S. 99
More, Thomas 91
Morris, W. *xi,* 89, 97, 100, 106–12, 124, 126, 130, 148, 150, 154–5
Morris–Susuki, T. 74
Morrison, J. 118
Morton, A. L. 109
Mosbacher, M. 81
Mouffe, C. 49
multinational corporations *x*, 66–8, 84, 86, 155
mutual aid 95

Nair, K. 140
News from Nowhere xi, 106–12
Nielsen, K. 46
Northcott, J. 69
Novak, M. 34
Nove, A. 39

Offe, C. 63
Ollman, B. 102
O'Sullivan, P. 110
Owen, R. 22, 92, 97
ownership *viii*, 41, 75, 144–5
  common *vii, xi*, 22–3, 121–3
  private, 15–16, 31

Paczuska, A. 90
Paine, Tom 92

Paris Commune *xi*, 29, 93
Peasants Revolt *xi*, 91
Peet, R. 34, 113
Pepper, D. 56, 88
Perrin, D. 53, 136, 141, 145
Pierson, C. 97
Pilger, J. 49
Plant, S. E. 61
Porritt, J. 86
poverty *ix*, 28, 34–5, 46–7, 51, 57, 79, 118, 133
power *viii, ix*, 17–19, 28–9, 37, 59, 74, 149
privatisation 57, 73, 76
production *vii–viii, xi*, 14–16, 22–6, 28, 59, 83, 101, 104, 123
  for use xii, 36, 108, 111, 128–34, 157
profit *vii, x, xii*, 24, 33, 57, 80, 125, 128, 147
  system 21, 35, 40, 43, 46, 52, 55, 61, 72, 76, 79, 91
property (private) *viii*, 18, 22, 82, 107

Reagan, R. 63
Redwood, J. 66
reformism *xi*, 36–44, 52, 55–6, 60, 65, 103, 113–20, 159
Reich, K. B. 38
Renton, D. 46
revolution *vii–xii*, 21, 27, 52–8, 68, 82, 103, 113–20, 147, 149, 152, 156, 159
Rheingold, H. 71
Ricardo 22
Rifkin, J. 44–5, 144–5
Ritzer, G. 41, 153
Robinson, J. 80–1
Rodley, G. 71
Rueschemeyer, D. 62

Sahlins, M. 15
Saint–Simon 22, 92
Sale, K. 70
Sanderson, S. K. 15
Sampson, A. 66–7, 84
Schor, J. 45
Schweikart, D. 33, 40
Schumann, H. 47, 76
Scott, W. R. 50, 132
Seabrook, J. 45, 157
Seldon, A. 31–2
Shaw, G. B. 98
Sherman, H. J. 69
Shutt, H. 117–8
Silk, L. 48
Silk, M. 48
Singer, D. 151, 155
Singer, M. 38
Singer, P. 27
Singman, J. L. 19
Slaughter, S. 74
slavery *vii–viii*, 18–9, 33, 90
Smith, Adam 47
Smith, K. 20, 54
Snooks, G. D. 14
Social Democratic Federation *vii*, 29, 87, 93, 156
social democracy *vii*, 29, 87, 93, 156
socialism *vii–viii, x–xi*, 27, 42, 55, 57, 61, 69, 89–159
  actually existing *viii, x*, 60, 121
  scientific 22
  utopian 22, 92
Socialist Party of Great Britain 53, 88, 93, 135–6, 139, 141, 143, 156
Soros, G. 37, 42
South Africa 46, 66–7
Soviet Union 31, 33, 52, 59–61, 86, 93, 97, 103, 151
Sowell, T. 22–3
Spartacus 90
sport 39, 71, 77, 140
Stalker, G. 131
Standage, T. 67
Staples, W. G. 81
Stratman, D. 28, 54, 77
Sutcliffe, B. 61, 110

Talbott, S. L. 70
tax(es) 19, 38, 61–2, 120
Taylor, A. 85
technology *viii, x*, 24, 33, 48, 69–71, 75, 81, 84, 148
Teeple, G. 38
television 28, 41, 47, 69–71, 73, 75–6, 82, 144

Thatcher, M. 33, 63
third way *ix*, 40–1
Third World 32, 48, 69–70, 98, 145, 148
Thomas, G. 23
Thompson, E. P. 111
Thompson, N. E. 95
Thompson, V. E. 144
Titmus, R. 95
Tomlinson, A. 45
trade unions 29, 114, 137
Trainer, T. 42
training *xii*, 72–3
Tressell, R. 89, 94
Trotskyism 29
Turner, B. S. 49

unemployment 24, 47–8, 51, 53–4, 69, 92, 137
USA 33, 36, 38–9, 42, 45–6, 76

Veal, A. J. 154
Venable, V. 19, 22
violence *xi*, 108, 112, 152
virtual reality 71, 144

Wachtel, P. 51, 55, 57
Walker, A. 33, 99
Wallace, I. 18
Walzer, M. 97
war(s) *xi*, 24, 125, 137
wealth *vii–viii, xi*, 17, 19, 24, 32, 46, 67, 79, 85, 111, 122–3
Weiss, L. 68
welfare *ix*, 40, 48, 50, 63, 115
White, G. 98
Wildavsky, A. 38
Wilde, Oscar *xi*, 94
Wood, E. A. 27, 63
Wood, E. M. 68
Worster, D. 85
Wright, A. 119

Zinn, H. 94